THE MENTOR THAT MATTERS
Stories of Transformational Teachers,
Role Models & Heroes

Volume 1

ANTHOLOGIES FROM STORIES OF YOU BOOKS

Stories of Inspiration:
Historical Fiction Edition

Stories of Inspiration:
Mystery Fiction Edition

The Message that Matters:
Wisdom for the Future from Lessons of the Past

Love, Loss, Legacy, and Life:
Stories from America's Extraordinary Hospices

Heart, Hope, and Healing:
Stories from America's Extraordinary Hospitals

www.storiesofyou.org

THE MENTOR THAT MATTERS
Stories of Transformational Teachers,
Role Models & Heroes

Volume 1

EDITED BY SUZANNE FOX
SERIES EDITOR, ANDY FOX

STORIES OF YOU BOOKS

STORIES OF YOU BOOKS
Post Office Box 691175
Vero Beach, FL 32969-1175
772.539.2904
www.storiesofyou.org
support@storiesofyou.org

*The Mentor That Matters: Stories of Transformational Teachers,
Role Models & Heroes, Volume 1*

Book design by cj Madigan
Cover photograph by © Csaba Peterdi through www.istockphoto.com.

For information on bulk sales and other special programs, contact Stories of You Books at support@storiesofyou.org.

Dedicated to
our mentors,
who help make us the best we can be

And in grateful memory
of the editors' first mentors,
Saul and Patricia Fox:
always remembered,
always appreciated

Make the most of yourself, for that is all there is of you.

—Ralph Waldo Emerson

Don't ask what the world needs. Ask what makes you come alive, and go do it. Because what the world needs is people who have come alive.

—Howard Thurman

The trouble with learning from experience is that you never graduate.

—Doug Larsen

A self-taught man usually has a poor teacher and a worse student.

— Henny Youngman

A man only learns in two ways, one by reading, and the other by association with smarter people.

—Will Rogers

I have come to believe that a great teacher is a great artist and that there are as few as there are any other great artists. Teaching might even be the greatest of the arts since the medium is the human mind and spirit.

—John Steinbeck

There's a genius in all of us.

—Albert Einstein

To see things in the seed—that is genius.

—Lao-Tzu

CONTENTS

ANDY FOX

PREFACE
Stories of *Mentors, Stories* as *Mentors*

Though elements of its roots are likely even more ancient, the word "mentor" as we know it was introduced and spread in stories. Homer's epic poem, *The Odyssey,* probably dating back to the 8th or 9th century B.C.E., is commonly credited with the introduction of the word. In *The Odyssey,* King Odysseus departs for the Trojan War, entrusting his old friend Mentor with keeping order in his household. Surprisingly, given the modern meaning of Mentor's name, *The Odyssey* makes no explicit reference to Odysseus asking Mentor to teach, guide, or protect Odysseus's son Telemachus.

It goes without saying that while Odysseus survives the war, his journey home is far longer and more complex than planned. Mentor's actual role, and his ability to fulfill it, is also complicated. As a human being he is, to say the least, ineffective. Notwithstanding Mentor's ostensibly caretaking presence, with the King presumed dead Odysseus' household is overrun by unscrupulous suitors courting his wife and attempting to seize his kingdom, while Telemachus—the future king and heir to the throne—becomes anxious and disempowered. When Mentor offers Telemachus anything like mentorship in the way we understand it today, it is only because the goddess Athena assumes his human guise. Speaking from Mentor's form and in his voice, this powerful deity assures Telemachus that she will stand beside him, protecting him and his interests.

Viewing *The Odyssey* as a story of mentorship, the fact that a goddess must intervene into human affairs to achieve an even reasonably effective outcome is not encouraging. Looked at metaphorically, however, the story becomes more powerful. Perhaps it suggests that when we take on the role of the mentor, we access the most godlike aspects of ourselves: our deepest wisdom, our highest aspirations, and our most profound impact on others. Great mentors are fully and even fallibly human, it may be saying, yet they are also graced, at least in their best moments, with divine inspiration.

According to an essay entitled "Homer's Mentor: Duties Fulfilled or Misconstrued?" by scholar Andy Roberts, it is a story much later than *The Odyssey*—the popular French book *Les Adventures de Telemaque*, first published in 1699—which resurrected the term "mentor" from relative obscurity and depicted a role closer to that of "mentor" as we understand it today. In this imitation and continuation of the Odyssey, Roberts explains, Mentor appears as a person who is actually charged with the role of counselor, protector, nurturer, and advisor, and who performs those roles well. The book's author, François Fenelon (or, to give him his full name, François de Salignac de La Mothe-Fenelon) was regarded as a great educator and tutor, giving him the hands-on expertise necessary to write a compelling description of mentorship. Becoming the most widely reprinted book of the 18th century, *Les Adventures de Telemaque* put its more specific, more successful vision of mentorship in front of an extraordinarily wide audience. In fact, Roberts suggests, it is probably thanks to Fenelon that the word "mentor" appeared in the English language for the first time in 1750.

While depictions of mentorship have been a constant ever since, the mentoring they portray is typically provided by figures playing familiar, pre-existing roles. Parents, and parent figures such as grandparents, uncles and aunts, and guardians; spiritual guides such as priests, rabbis, shamans, ministers and gurus; saints and divine beings; tutors, governesses and teachers; royalty, aristocrats, politicians and other leaders: all provide recognizable forms of mentoring throughout centuries of stories across all continents. They just do it in the course of playing roles that already exist for other purposes. To state this differently, all of these figures are in effect mentors, but most often because some element of guidance is inherent in a role they already play.

In stories from the past 75 or so years, however, that has changed. Mentorship is still of course widely portrayed within the context of existing supportive roles. But more and more stories now depict mentoring in and of itself, purveyed by figures who may not have any built-in reason to mentor—and in some cases, no existing experience in or gifts for doing so. Animals, children, servants, therapists, and peers who act as mentors have appeared in growing numbers. Antiheroes including criminals and others on society's fringe are sometimes seen as offering wise mentoring even to those with no shady intentions. Professionals traditionally understood as asking or taking rather than giving, such as employers, more and more commonly appear offering mentorship's transformative gifts; specialists once evoked as playing a single or highly limited service, such as doctors or athletic coaches, are shown as imparting broader wisdom and more extended or extensive nurturance. The process of mentoring appears more and more centrally in plots and storylines, and protagonists are more likely than ever before to be considered heroes solely because of their mentoring gifts.

The limitations of space that constrain me here, and my eagerness to let you move on to enjoy this volume's own remarkable mentoring stories, prevent me from naming more than a very few examples. But with the understanding that these skim only the shallowest surface of a deep and teeming sea, let me say that instances of what I describe above include films as diverse as the Star Wars series and the animated films of Disney and Pixar, *Chariots of Fire* and *The Karate Kid*, *Good Will Hunting* and *Driving Miss Daisy*; television series built around mentoring such as *The Profit*, *American Idol* and *The Biggest Loser*; and thousands of books from J.K. Rowling's Harry Potter series to Kathryn Stockett's *The Help*, Mitch Albom's *Tuesdays with Morrie* to Azar Nafisi's *Reading Lolita in Tehran*. In the field of business and performance specifically, stories of mentoring have become an immensely popular and enduring staple. Ken Blanchard's *The One-Minute Manager* and *Raving Fans*, Spencer Johnson's *The Present*, Bob Burg and John David Mann's *The Go-Giver*, and Mark Sanborn's *The Fred Factor* each offer wisdom in the form of a single mentoring narrative. Numerous other business books focus or touch on mentoring using stories in the form of case histories. Given that longitudinal studies demonstrating replicable, empirical benefits from mentoring are scant and a single commonly accepted definition of exactly what mentoring is remains wanting, businesses themselves have been less willing to invest in mentoring efforts than readers are eager to buy books about it. Nevertheless, the visibility and success of business-related mentoring stories is striking.

The combined ubiquity and popularity of all of these modern stories of mentoring suggests three important truths. First, that the concept of the entirely "self-made man" or woman has had its day and any stigma associated with needing mentoring is disappearing if not gone. Today, phenomenally successful business titans, acclaimed performing artists, entertainment celebrities, and sports champions (such as Bill Gates, Mark Zuckerberg, Michael Bloomberg, Quincy Jones, Meryl Streep, Oprah Winfrey, and Joe Montana, to name just a few) have begun to proudly recognize their mentors (Warren Buffett, Steve Jobs, William R. Salomon, Ray Charles, Joseph Papp, Maya Angelou, and Bill Walsh, respectively) as being instrumental to their eventual success. Having a transformative mentor is no longer considered to make one's achievements any less exciting, unique or admirable. In fact, it is nearly as "cool"—and otherwise impressive—to volunteer to be a "mentee" as it is to become a mentor.

Second, the explosion of mentoring stories in our culture affirms that mentorship is a surprisingly dramatic act. You might not think that teaching and guiding someone sounds like the stuff that best-sellers and blockbusters are made of...but you would be wrong. As it is understood today, the act of effective mentoring leads to change: change that enhances the "mentee's" authenticity, sense of direction, and power with satisfying and even startling results. Far from being a dull sideline to a dramatic tale, such transformation is itself the stuff of compelling story.

Finally, the popularity of mentor stories suggests that our culture is increasingly fascinated, even obsessed, by stories that reveal the details and dynamics of mentorship. It is beyond the purview of this preface or this book to explore all of the possible reasons for this fascination. But I would point out that a perfect storm of socioeconomic and cultural factors has eaten into the time and energy traditional sources of guidance can devote to their mentoring roles. Parenting time has dwindled as single-parent and two-income families have become more prevalent and extended families have scattered, hence making grandparents, aunts, uncles and others less available as parent substitutes. Reductions in school funding have cut staff and extracurricular programs, while factors including mandated curricula and larger class sizes have constrained teachers' ability to form unique, transformative bonds with individual students. Corporate downsizing—fueled by fierce global competition, ever-accelerating technological innovation, and the disruptions of ongoing global financial crises—has similarly reduced the freedom of supervisors, managers and other business to invest significant resources in nurturing an employee's wisdom and talent beyond what is needed for the job. Smaller houses of worship have closed and mega-versions have multiplied, making the once highly personalized religious mentorship available in the community more rare. The explosion of new fields such as life coaching makes up for some of these gaps, but mentors paid solely as such remain too costly for the majority of those seeking guidance to afford.

Yet while *less* mentoring is likely to be available from familiar social, educational, religious and professional structures, our increasingly complicated lives demand *more* astute and experienced guidance than ever. A vastly enlarged array of choices—social, geographical, religious, cultural, personal, and professional—faces young people. The need for re-education or even reinvention is an increasingly common, even an urgent feature of later life. Just as traditional sources of "real life" mentorship falter, it seems, we are more than ever in need of the wisdom, insight, protection and direction that great mentors offer.

Fewer automatically available mentors, more need for them: This, I would hazard, may be why stories of mentoring have become so prevalent, so diverse and so beloved in our culture. Whether purveyed as film or novel, blog or business guide, television show or TED talk, stories of mentorship are widely accessible, relatively if not completely affordable, available in variations that fit almost every circumstance and need, and, at their best, unforgettably powerful and transformative.

Centuries before the advent of written history, orally transmitted stories of mentoring like *The Odyssey* taught their listeners practical strategies for mastering human challenges and inspired them to reach for the excellence of heroes and even gods. Today, an immensely rich and diverse body of stories and narratives does the same. Some explicitly portray mentors and mentorship; some teach and counsel, protect and nurture in less direct or specific ways. But all nevertheless help us solve our darkest problems, encourage us to reach our greatest and most shining goals, and represent the power that can be harnessed when one human being guides and helps another.

In fact, you might even say that stories have become—indeed, may always have been—humanity's most powerful mentors of all.

Andy Fox
Pinehurst, North Carolina
October 2016

SUZANNE FOX

INTRODUCTION
A Transformation of Mentors

While working on this book, I found myself wondering what a group of mentors is called. If many lions are a pride, many owls a parliament and many butterflies a flutter (that latter term seems almost too delightful to be true, but *National Geographic* assures me that it is), what are many mentors? I toyed with a *teaching* of mentors and a *dialogue* of mentors before hitting on one that seemed right.

A *transformation* of mentors, I think, pretty much says it all.

In his Preface to this book, my twin brother and publishing partner Andy Fox—a transformative mentor of my own—speaks briefly about the power of mentoring stories. Here, let me speak with equal brevity about how the particular transformation of mentors you will find in *The Mentor That Matters* was assembled.

First, I should emphasize the importance of the supplemental nouns in the book's subtitle: teachers, role models and heroes. (We use the latter word in a gender-neutral sense to avoid the sometimes limiting connotations of "heroine.") Had front-book-cover space and the constraints of marketing permitted, we might have added *inspirations, examples, influences,* and no doubt other terms as well. Our interest did not lie in mentorship in any narrowly defined or technical sense, but rather in the broader, more varied, and to our minds, more interesting ways in which one person transforms another. Hence, the essays here encompass both figures that might fit a narrow definition of "mentor" and those—such as favorite authors and Jesus—that do not.

Equally important, we made vigorous efforts to include contributors representing a diversity of professions, locations, ages and so on. The constraints of time and the vagaries of contributor availability led to unexpected gaps and clusters. This collection ended up including several contributors each from the fields of science, business, healing and writing, for example, but does not have a contributor who is a rabbi or a politician even though we reached out to both; similarly, it lacks a mentor drawn from athletic coaching, a fascination of Andy's, or from visual arts, a lifelong love of mine. The professions and relationships of the mentors discussed also clustered in unpredictable ways: we received multiple essays about mothers and also about fathers, but none about mentoring siblings or spouses. Ultimately, the sheer variety of human beings who have either been or had mentors may doom any hopes for perfect diversity or assortment from the start. Having conceived *The Mentor That Matters* as a series rather than a single volume, we look forward to broadening our range of contributors and mentors in future books.

In a few instances, we were able to create linkages between essays. Peter Raven writes about G. Ledyard Stebbins; Stebbins writes about Theodosius Dobzhansky. Lydia McGranahan celebrates Marilyn Bousquin, while Marilyn Bousquin honors Gail Collins-Ranadive. As these connections suggest, mentoring at its best is a linked chain in which each person who is mentored by another goes on to mentor others in his or her turn.

Once contributors agreed to participate, we gave them the freedom to decide for themselves which, and which kind, of mentor they wished to write about. It felt essential to let contributors speak authentically of the mentoring experiences that meant most to them, rather than to nudge them toward choices that fit our own wish for variety. The only exceptions occurred late in the gathering process, when the sufficiency of pieces about both mothers and fathers that I mention above led us to take those options off the essayistic table.

Similarly, we imposed no restrictions on an essayist's choices of focus, approach or literary style beyond an insistence on first-person voice and a few fundamental, even foundational expectations: that respect for people's dignity and privacy be maintained, to name one crucial example. The majority of contributors wrote the essays that appear under their names in this book. Approximately one-quarter of them was interviewed by either Andy or myself, after which the contributor revised and approved an essay built from the transcript of our conversation. A handful of essays, noted on the Prior Publications page at the back of the book, are reprinted with grateful thanks to the blogs, periodicals, and other sources on which they first appeared.

Some of these stories are playful, some are pensive, and some are fierce and even challenging. Some reference mentors, such as parents or bosses, to whom many readers may relate; others focus on mentors who will have a narrower appeal. We do not expect all stories to resonate for all readers, nor endorse any particular mentoring or learning choice. Instead, we hope this collection affirms the many and colorful paths that teaching and learning follow; prompts new thinking about the nature of growth and change; and celebrates both the sparkling differences and the warm common bonds that characterize human stories. Our goal at Stories of You Books is to explore the truths that can be found at the intersection of many experiences; we hope that the diverse perspectives in this book will themselves provide a kind of mentoring that inspires you to think about the gifts of your past as well as the possibilities of your future.

The 41 individuals that contributed to this volume gave us their time, energy and wisdom without any compensation for doing so other than a pair of free copies of the finished book. *The Mentor That Matters* literally could not exist without their generosity. If I may yet again invent a collective noun, to this transformation of contributors we give a gratitude, a grace, a reverence, even an exaltation of thanks.

Suzanne Fox
Vero Beach, Florida
October 2016

LEAH ABRAHAMS

on Mary Jane Grunsfeld

I walked through the smoke-filled secretarial pool and entered the office of Mary Jane. Such a common name for such an un-common woman! Mary Jane Grunsfeld sat quietly behind her paper-strewn desk, smoke wafting up from a cigarette burning in her huge ashtray. Her lined face was clean of make-up; her eyes were covered by large eyeglass frames and her greyish hair was pulled into a casual bun at the back of her head. Her gravelly voice welcomed me to my first day as a clerk in the Michigan Avenue research department of a small but competitive ad agency in my hometown of Chicago. It was June 1962. Think *Mad Men* transplanted to Michigan Avenue—*Mich Men?*—and you'll picture it. The secre-taries had bouffant hairdos; the company was primarily populated by men in shirtsleeves, jackets and ties; and glasses of scotch rested on their desks after 5pm—and on Mary Jane's, too.

I had just graduated from Northwestern University and was to start graduate school in sociology at Washington University in St. Louis in three months, a fact that I conveniently, although guiltily, concealed in order to get a summer job. Mary Jane was the second in command in the agency's research department. I later discovered that she had never finished college, but after going through an early marriage and divorce and serving as Director of the Clearing House of the American Council on Race Relations, she had joined this agency and proceeded to manage its everyday market research on ads and products.

Although I had conducted attitude surveys for college courses and had a special interest in attitude change, I had never worked in an advertising agency. Mary Jane taught me everything I needed to do my job well: how to define clearly what we were trying to test; how to set up a survey and decide whether it should be telephone or face-to-face; how to word questions, analyze results and communicate clearly to the client. She also made sure I knew how to check up on the accuracy of our surveyors' time sheets. Did they really make those calls?

Mary Jane took a liking to me–even though I was new to advertising, I think she recognized my hunger to learn and potential to grow—and gave me assignments that often angered the secretaries with whom I shared space. They were typing boring dictation after several years of employment and there I was, the newcomer, creating surveys…arranging for outside companies to make phone calls asking about "our" salad dressing, "our" brand of laundry soap and "our" brand of liquor…not to mention staying late and getting to eat take-out from the famous London House restaurant in our building. One secretary barely talked to me. Another girl was a bit friendlier and let me mooch three cigarettes each day. A third took me to get my hair done stylishly and encouraged regular manicures. I was in awe of this new environment and rather unsophisticated about the working world; I learned a lot about it from these peers. Mary Jane was basically unadorned and very different from the others. I think I really identified more with her, as I didn't wear much makeup, had outside intellectual interests as she did, and was raised by an immigrant working mother who didn't get manicures or drink socially and an idealistic father whose clientele as a lawyer was too often *pro bono.*

Meanwhile, Mary Jane corrected my surveys to make them analyzable and admitted that as she aged (she was in her mid-fifties), she kept changing the age categories on our surveys so that her current age was never in the oldest one. Mary Jane would occasionally talk about her life as a young daughter of a prominent Chicago family, as their child with a rebellious flair. She played the viola in quartets, went to the opera and the symphony, and after dropping out of college was basically self-educated. I found out later that she was also a Communist sympathizer during the dangerous time of the investigations sponsored by the House Un-American Activities Committee, carrying pamphlets in her viola case to secret meetings. In retrospect, the fact of her working in that most capitalistic of professions as a market and advertising researcher seems somewhat ironic.

I loved Mary Jane for her competence, independence and calm manner. Just the way a teacher might be hardest on the students with the most promise, when Mary Jane corrected me I felt privileged. She did have a designated research assistant, Caroline, a recent graduate of the University of Chicago, and I was never quite sure of myself when I interacted with her; I felt she thought I was an upstart.

This changed somewhat at the end of the summer when I went to tell Mary Jane that I was leaving for graduate school. "Why don't you wait a year?" she asked. Her query reinforced my sense that I still had a lot to learn and told me that she valued my work enough to want to continue to teach me. As I had no compelling reason to have to start grad school, I decided to stay. (To be honest, I was also involved in a blooming romance locally and liked the idea of keeping it going!) So, as a newly appointed second research assistant, I began to collaborate with the other researcher. At the same time, I started a campaign to get the resentful secretary to like me (eventually she did).

My decision to stay on for another year was the right one because what I learned was invaluable to me in future positions—even more worthwhile than the courses I later took in grad school. Mary Jane was always supportive but demanding as she guided me in the craft and art of market research and good writing. I was learning about focus groups (a new concept in those days) and conducting them in consumer homes. I was learning about consumer loyalty, surveyor behavior and the mores of advertising industry executives. For example, Ingrid, a new secretary who looked and dressed like the character Joan Holloway on *Mad Men*, was brought on. Her figure and sexy manner immediately became the subject of watercooler or coffee breaks for many of the married men in the agency, as well as the other secretaries. Ironically, she ended up with the confirmed bachelor chief financial officer, half her height, twice her age and many times richer.

I never lost touch with Mary Jane, although life and love took me away from her and Chicago. I went on to graduate school, marriage, children and always a job in which I applied what I had learned from Mary Jane. Her wedding present to me was a 17th-century map of the Holy Land. A reminder of my faith, my year of college study in Israel, and my friendship with her, it is still one of my most valued possessions. As I look back on my work with her I realize that she was a mentor in the best sense. From her I learned not only how to be a professional researcher, but also the values of being honest, trying to find the best way to uncover the truth of a customer-product relationship, and communicating ethically with consumers and clients.

Mary Jane understood me and used that understanding to guide me. Today I am a personal historian, helping my clients to document their family stories as a legacy for future generations. Many of my insights into human behavior and my interviewing and writing skills I owe to Mary Jane Grunsfeld, and therefore writing this brief essay and reminiscing about our relationship brings me great pleasure.

Boston-area resident **LEAH ABRAHAMS** is the creator and owner of Mixed Media Memoirs LLC, a publishing company. She is a personal historian, writing, editing and/or creating memoir books and oral history videos for her clients, some for private distribution and some for sale to the public. She also shows her fine art photography in Boston-area venues. Leah was born and raised in Chicago; she has a B.A. from Northwestern University and an M.A. from the University of Wisconsin at Madison. She worked in the public sector evaluating government-funded programs and then in market research in the financial services industry. Leah has been honored for leadership in voluntary organizations in her former community of Green Bay, Wisconsin and is a member of the Association of Personal Historians. Find Leah online at www.mixedmediamemoirs.com.

J. DAVID BEAM

on Jesus

My mom worked in the church, so even before I was ever aware of it, Jesus has always been part of my life. I don't feel like I chose Jesus as my mentor; I feel like he was given to me. How Jesus was presented to me as a child helped me grow. Since I can remember, there was that message that Jesus loved me unconditionally; God's love was always with me no matter what. That truth was formative for me as a child and remains so today.

Obviously, my understanding of Jesus grew as my faith grew. As I matured in my faith and in life, my understanding of him matured as well. His mentorship has looked different through different seasons: it's continuously changing along with me.

For me, everything starts with the realization that Jesus knows me, cares about me, and is present in my life. The intimacy of the relationship is the greatest gift of all. It's the relationship with Jesus that allows for growth. That's one of the things that allows me to write about him as a mentor. It all goes back to, "Jesus loves me, this I know," or "Jesus knows me, this I love." Both are true. That's a very humbling thing.

Jesus's teaching was incarnational; he lived out the truth that he embodied. His mentorship invites me to recognize what God's love looked like for him and replicate that however I can in my own life. Two key questions for me are: "How do we live out God's love in the world?" and, "How do you live out your faith?" Jesus's mentorship continually helps reveal those things to me.

Jesus' great teachings are important, but I don't think you can reduce his mentorship to a set of teachings. He lived out all his teaching in his life. Jesus never set down a list of hard-and-fast laws or wrote his era's equivalent of a book, let alone a "Top Ten" list of ways to follow God. Instead, he said, "Come and follow me," to the disciples. Yet Jesus provided the constant, abiding presence of God that strengthened them and gave direction, hope, meaning, and significance to their lives, as he does for mine.

It's been written that over his years of ministry, Jesus asked his followers over 300 questions and only directly answered three of them. His teaching was inductive. He would lead people in the struggle for great understanding of who God is by asking profound questions. He prompted people to dive deep into their own souls and to wrestle with profound mysteries. But he also walked with them as they began to find the often-elusive answers, present through all of the searching and struggle.

We often think of Jesus very personally, but seldom in terms of his personality. Jesus wasn't some sort of distant mythical or divine creature who was above emotion. He was fully God, fully man.

Throughout the Gospels, I sense the deep passion he brings to all aspects of his ministry. Grieving the loss of his friend, Lazarus, for example, Jesus was moved to tears. There are stories about him reaching out to those suffering on the fringes of society that show his compassion for these people was so great you almost feel the weight of his heart breaking. And there are stories of times when he saw injustice and got mad. When he saw something that was profoundly wrong, he didn't hold back: turning over tables in the Temple, for instance, or calling the Pharisees a "brood of vipers." All of those stories—and others like them in the Gospels—are so beautiful to me. They testify not only to his ministry and mission but also demonstrate the full of breadth of his humanity. When I grieve or get angry, I know he did the same—his humanity constantly invites us into those places that engage us most viscerally through all the seasons and situations of our lives.

I might add that I can identify with the humanity of Jesus's disciples as well. It's humorous and also moving that to the very end of the Gospels, they never quite "get" what's going on. These people who have been closest to him seemingly can't put two and two together, so to speak. We see the disciples' profound struggles, their lapses, their uncertainty. Yet, after Easter, we see how emboldened they became in their faith—in the Book of Acts, we read about how they're out healing people and starting churches. We wonder, "Are these the same guys that just didn't get it a year and a half ago?"

For me, there's something really powerful about that. Among other things, it reminds me that we can be transformed no matter how fallible, how unclear, how much a "work in progress" we always are. It's reassuring, too, because it reminds me that faith has never been the accumulation of right answers or impeccable behavior. Instead, it's seeking out and following after Jesus, whom we believe is the truth. All of that allows me to have more grace with myself in the many moments when I make a mistake or have to admit in a conversation or Bible study that "I don't know."

My mentor lived over 2,000 years ago. But Jesus said, "I am the truth," and while the context for it might alter I don't think the truth changes with time. If Jesus were to preach here this Sunday morning, I would fully anticipate him getting up and delivering the Sermon on the Mount again. I think he'd be just as active in today's context as he was all those millennia ago, although the questions he'd ask and the particular acts of cruelty or injustice that might infuriate him might be different. I believe Jesus is always challenging us in new ways to reconcile our faith and our actions with God's truth. For me, even though we talk about Christ as a historical figure, he is still an extraordinarily active force in the world.

It's impossible for me to differentiate the impact of Jesus on my personal life from his impact on me as a minister. At one point Jesus says, "My burden is easy and my yoke is light," yet he also says, "Pick up your cross and follow me." For me, discipleship sometimes feels incredibly demanding, yet I feel a deep sense of joy through it, too. People will post a "No visitors" sign on a hospital door, and yet that doesn't apply to ministers, because they want us to come and say a prayer. A couple wants to marry, a child is born, someone dies, a community suffers—and often we're the first ones the family or community calls. Being present at life's most sacred moments is at once so searing, and so significant. Jesus reminds us that God's love is for everyone; personally and professionally, that's a message I just can't hear—or share—enough.

How do you quantify Jesus' mentorship? With a lot of mentors, you've got points of comparison: you might have one extraordinary teacher but also three inadequate ones. I don't have any comparison to some other religious leader that I followed for a season. Instead, to quote Revelation 22:13, for me Jesus is "the Alpha and the Omega, the First and the Last, the Beginning and the End."

The value of mentorship is often measured in how and how much the "mentee" changes. With Jesus, that's hard if not impossible to quantify. He's not a coach charged with helping us shave precious seconds off a race time; he works with the totality of who we are. I know I've grown in following him, but I can't analyze crisply how much, or exactly in what ways.

Similarly, my faith itself is the reason I can't pin down precisely where Jesus's mentorship will bring me in the future. Two of my favorite hymns in the United Methodist Church Hymnal touch on this. The opening of Number 382 says "Thou art the potter, I am the clay"; the ending of Number 515 says, "at the last, a victory, unrevealed until its season, something God alone can see." But perhaps John 3:8 expresses it most beautifully: "The wind blows where it chooses, and you hear the sound of it, but you do not know where it comes from or where it goes. So it is with everyone who is born of the Spirit."

Originally from Raleigh, **REVEREND J. DAVID BEAM** serves as the Senior Pastor at Pinehurst United Methodist Church in Pinehurst, North Carolina. David is a graduate of the Wesley Foundation at Wake Forest University and Emory University's Candler School of Theology. He has been married to Carolyn, a freelance medical and science writer, for over nine years and they have two young children, Adele and Joseph. In his free time, David enjoys Wake Forest sports, reading, riding his bike, traveling, watching movies, dining out, visiting with friends and family, and spending time with Carolyn, their children, and their high-maintenance dog, Sophie. Find many of David's sermons at www.pinehurstumc.org/sermons.

KIM BECKER

on Millard Fuller

I have had so many amazing people pour insight and inspiration into me during my life that it is difficult to choose a single person that I would consider my most transformative mentor. This piece is about a man who inspired me with the legacy that he left on this earth, by the work that he did and through the words of wisdom he spoke to me. They changed my way of thinking and propelled our organization forward in a way we never thought possible.

I am a true believer in "modeling." If I want to know or learn how to do something, I find someone who has already done it and model after them. So that's what I did when my husband and I started Hello Gorgeous!, our nonprofit organization providing complimentary professional makeovers and cosmetic education to women battling all cancers. Starting a business is no easy task. Starting a nonprofit can be tedious. Starting a nonprofit that you want to take national can seem like a huge, unattainable feat.

I knew in my heart I was supposed to embrace this dream and reach as many women as possible. So I sought out the guidance of someone that had already attained something similar. I had a client who would talk about a man whose name I hadn't heard before. This couple saw him frequently, donating their time and skill performing corporate tax services to his nonprofit organization. His name was Millard Fuller and he was the founder of Habitat for Humanity.

Habitat for Humanity builds homes for the less fortunate. The world vision of the organization is to ensure that everyone has a decent place to live. Houses are built mostly by volunteers, no profit is built into their costs, and no interest is charged on the loans for them. My client thought that we would be able to gain some valuable insight from Millard Fuller. Building houses doesn't sound like pampering women with cancer, but he had accomplished something similar to what we were hoping to achieve, and on a scale that really made a difference.

One Friday afternoon in May 2007, my husband Michael was running errands when his cell phone rang. The Southern-accented voice on the other end of the line asked to speak with Michael. After my husband responded that he was Michael, the Southern gentleman introduced himself as Millard Fuller. Michael was dumbfounded. He asked if we could call him back so that I could be on the phone as well, to listen and ask my questions. Millard said, "Of course," and they set a time to chat later in the day. Michael called me right away to tell me what had happened. We were both pretty stunned, to say the least. So we sat down and wrote out what we thought were the most important questions to ask a nonprofit legend, so that we could use wisely every minute we had with him.

We called Millard back a few hours later with our list of questions. He was a wonderful man and offered so much information. We were on the phone with him for over an hour. I felt like it would take me a month to process everything he had said. I queried him about creating a board of directors as well as about how to grow from a local to an international nonprofit. I told him our big dream was to pamper a half-million women each year. I told him what our Mobile Day Spa would look like and how it would pull up just a few feet from a woman's door and make her feel like a queen for a day during a time when she didn't feel very special. When I finished unfolding this beyond-belief vision, I asked Millard a question that still resonates with me today. I asked him, "How much money do I need in the bank to really get this rolling? What do you think?"

"Kim, you would be really silly to start without a dollar."

His answer completely caught me off guard. Then I got the gist: we only needed a dollar to start.

He continued, "Kim, these women don't care where you take care of them. You could give them a manicure in a back alley over a trashcan. They just want to be taken care of. You just need to start." I was speechless, which does not happen very often. But I wasn't sure what to do next. I had my mind set on raising the funds to get the Mobile Day Spa first and only then beginning our work. He was suggesting I start without them. What would that look like? Was it even possible?

Over the next few months, Michael and I took Millard's suggestion. Every Friday, we started performing surprise makeovers on women battling cancer in the salon we already owned. He was right; we just needed to start. As our efforts evolved, we were able to raise the funds to purchase our first Mobile Day Spa. Over the next year, we performed dozens of makeovers on women battling cancer, but we knew that what we could do on our own would never be enough to get to the millions of women who needed our help.

We remembered the seed that Millard had planted in us: "Just start." We used the knowledge we had gained performing makeovers in our salon to create a certification program that would engage existing salons in pampering the women battling cancer in their own communities. We now have Certified Hello Gorgeous! Affiliate Salons coast to coast, and we're still growing. And at each certification ceremony we conduct, we share the story of Millard Fuller and his influence on me and our organization. Millard passed away in 2009; as a small gesture to keep the legacy of his advice to us alive, we give each salon affiliate a symbolic $1.00 bill to start.

Because of that one 60-minute conversation, the Hello Gorgeous! Affiliate Program is now in 11 states. We have authored two books to encourage and inspire women battling cancer and added a second Mobile Day Spa to begin our fleet. We are creating online courses to educate hair stylists to guide women battling cancer to stay "Gorgeous!" and a program that helps beauty schools make students aware of the importance of empowering women with cancer. It has all grown from that one phone call.

I can't speak for Millard Fuller, but I can—and do—pass on the same suggestion that he gave us. If you have a big goal or a dream, find a dollar bill and just start. Conditions will never be perfect and available money will never feel like quite enough. Just start, and you'll probably be surprised by the way it all comes together.

Thank you, Millard.

KIM BECKER is the founder of Hello Gorgeous! of HOPE, a nonprofit organization that restores in women the beauty that cancer steals. Kim has been in the beauty industry as a salon owner and national educator for more than 25 years. A fundraiser, educator, public speaker, consultant and the face of Hello Gorgeous!, Kim has received the Spirit of Women and Daily Points of Light Awards. Kim's books are *Hello Gorgeous!: A Journey of Faith, Love and Hope,* a Mom's Choice Award winner, and *I Promise to Put My Lipstick on When I Get There,* for women battling cancer. Kim and her husband Michael have been married for over 20 years and thrive in Indiana with their son, Seth, and a pug named Sam. Find out more at www.hellogorgeous.org.

KEN BENEDICT

on William V. Burlingame

I met William V. Burlingame, Ph.D. in the fall of 1986. I was 23 and in the first year of my doctoral program in clinical psychology at the University of North Carolina at Chapel Hill. Probably in his mid-50s at the time, Dr. Burlingame was a Clinical Adjunct Professor and also the director of a long-term adolescent unit at the state psychiatric hospital where some of the graduate students in my program trained.

I probably would have ended up selecting UNC as my graduate school anyway, but reading Dr. Burlingame's brief biography in the faculty roster helped sway me. His area of interest was tersely presented as "residential treatment of adolescents," and working with teenagers was of major interest to me. I remember thinking something like, "I hope I can catch up with this guy." Fortunately, I did, and pretty quickly. Dr. Burlingame co-taught my first semester child psychopathology class. I then ended up spending three years on the adolescent unit he directed, the latter two electively. Finally, he became a member of my dissertation committee.

Dr. Burlingame wasn't necessarily considered one of those "gotta have" professors by most of my classmates, probably because he was viewed as a bit "old school" and had somewhat distant quality that some found difficult to read even though it appealed to me. So when I volunteered for both of my extra years working under him in the adolescent unit, the attitude of some of my classmates could be summed up as "Really? You're really going to do another year out there?" My answer was simple: "Definitely." Students before me who had taken the opportunity to work with him valued the experience greatly, and later earned some of the best internships in the country. Moreover, Dr. Burlingame was particularly knowledgeable about professional ethics and was the Chair of the State Licensing Board Committee, an indication of the high regard in which other practicing psychologists held him. I thought learning from him might be as inspiring as it would be challenging, and I was right.

Dr. Burlingame was an adjunct professor rather than a full-time academic and a Ph.D. rather than an M.D. From my viewpoint, he was a genuine, "true blue" psychologist who rolled up his sleeves to work every day with some of the most difficult kids in the state: a representative of the real world of clinical psychology rather than a permanent inhabitant of the academic ivory tower. I was impressed that he had obtained the directorship of a clinical unit as a Ph.D. in a traditionally M.D.-dominant culture. That told me that his adolescent unit was really about psychological counseling and therapy, and not merely medication management. All of this struck me as appealing and professionally heady, and that's exactly what it turned out to be.

Dr. Burlingame's style back then was a bit of a throwback to an earlier era—his wide ties and jacket lapels had a 1960s or 1970s look. He had an appealing face and for lack of a better word was cool-looking, reminding me of a mix between Neil Young and Roy Orbison. He didn't seem to care about status symbols but I remember that he drove a fairly nice sports car. He was clearly capable of appreciating a joke, but he wasn't naturally jocular. His typical manner was reflective and thoughtful, even wistful at times.

Getting to know Dr. Burlingame during our work at the adolescent unit was an intriguing but quite gradual process. Other than in the group therapy we conducted together on the adolescent unit, he never directly supervised me. His preference was not to teach directly, set specific goals, or provide much feedback. This could be frustrating but over time I came to appreciate the freedom. I felt that I was a welcome—and eventually valued—visitor in his "house," and that he respected me enough to trust me to make of it what I would.

Watching him in action was where the action was for me. When Dr. Burlingame said something, it mattered. He was an eloquent speaker, with a remarkable way of putting language and theory together that often left me a bit spellbound. His way of conducting even routine staff meetings was fascinating, particularly in his insightful, concise summaries of what was transpiring with various patients. He was masterful at managing discussions in group therapy sessions. Exchanges there frequently entailed a teenager spontaneously revealing a horrifying interpersonal trauma, usually for the first time in his or her life. Just as memorable to me were the pithy comments he would make as we departed from the office. One that became familiar was "That was pure gold." The other, often accompanying the first, was, "That never gets easy." The economy of words with which he commented on them made the experiences themselves feel even more sacrosanct in my mind.

It was observing Dr. Burlingame's work with highly disturbed adolescents that taught and inspired me most powerfully. In watching him, I realized that his presence, as much as any particular action or approach, was his most powerful tool. He was silent, serene, mostly still. There was a kind of mystery about him, some combination of what might have been distance, reserve, sadness, shyness, or all of those things. It's somewhat pat to describe him as a benign father-like figure to the teenagers we treated, but I think that's ultimately how he was regarded. I also had a subtle but unconfirmed impression that he was a member of the unofficial, unacknowledged club of people who knew suffering. That may have been one of the reasons that even deeply traumatized adolescent clients felt safe around him.

For all these reasons, he earned the kids' respect and didn't invoke the kind of oppositional dynamic that's so characteristic of adolescents. Even working with troubled teens who struggled fiercely with authority, he had no need to rely on power plays or manipulations of any kind. There was a genuineness to the way that he approached each teen as a fascinating and worthy soul and bore witness, often with minimal verbiage, to unimaginable trauma.

Over the course of the several years during which I worked with him, Dr. Burlingame and I gradually grew closer to and more trusting with each other. Ironically for a psychologist and psychologist-in-training who value bringing feelings into awareness and words, this was never directly acknowledged. Once, he invited me to join him at a bluegrass festival, where I remember getting drunk on cheap box wine. At a big social gathering at his home we connected over our similar musical tastes, particularly for the Grateful Dead. Those more lighthearted moments were a good antidote to the intensity of our working life, which so consistently took place around people in deep pain.

It's difficult to articulate the gratitude I feel for Dr. Burlingame's teaching and example. He had a formative, foundational and enduring impact on my professional development that was all the more valuable for coming so early in my career. Working under him confirmed and even strengthened my interest in working with adolescents, a core focus of my practice to this day. My involvement in forensic work stems directly from watching Dr. Burlingame present cases for which he was a court-appointed evaluator.

Training under Dr. Burlingame, I not only built an understanding of adolescent development but also grasped a way of being with them that is effective and even transformative. He modeled a way of sitting and bearing witness with someone who has been damaged in some way that doesn't elicit an automatic oppositional stance. That informs my work with adolescents and carries over to my work with other people who, for whatever set of upsetting reasons, struggle profoundly with trust and attachment, including traumatized adult patients and those whom I assess in jail or prison settings. When I have had the privilege of supervising psychologists—in practicum settings in graduate school and internship programs in teaching hospitals, among other situations—I always try to pass on what my mentor taught me about the power of creating an accepting, non-threatening, authentic and genuinely attentive presence to help those affected by trauma and other pervasive harm.

KEN BENEDICT is Founder and Co-Director of the Center for Psychology & Education, PLLC. He is a Licensed Psychologist and Certified Health Care Provider in North Carolina. Ken's areas of specialization include psychological, psychoeducational, and developmental neuropsychological assessment of students from three years of age into adulthood; legal evaluations; parent and school consultation; adolescent development; and individual and family therapy. He has years of experience working with students with a variety of challenges and enjoys consulting with private schools and testing agencies. Ken's undergraduate training in psychology was completed at Dartmouth College; he received his master's and doctoral degrees from the University of North Carolina at Chapel Hill and completed clinical internships and postdoctoral training at Harvard Medical School/Massachusetts General Hospital in Boston. Ken and his family live in Chapel Hill, North Carolina. Find out more at www.cpsyched.com.

MARILYN BOUSQUIN

on Gail Collins-Ranadive

In the fall of 1992, when I was 26 and wrenched from sleep night after night by irrepressible sobs I could not make sense of, I enrolled in a writing course called "Writing Re-creatively: A Spiritual Quest for Women." It was my habit, then, to write in composition notebooks while seated at an old pie hutch that still smelled faintly of flour.

I'd graduated from college in 1988 with an English degree and a conviction that I did not have a voice and therefore was not a "real writer." This was before Anita Hill awakened the culture to the term "sexual harassment," before I'd ever heard the term "date rape," before my college had a single women's studies course much less a women's studies program. Such landmark studies as Carol Gilligan's 1982 *In a Different Voice*, which drew attention to girls' loss of voice at adolescence, had not made it into the classrooms where I was learning to write.

In one of those classrooms a professor who wore tweed jackets taught creative writing. An acclaimed short story writer, he talked about Hemingway and Chekov and Tolstoy (a lot) and once, I re-member, he ranted because a student did not know the word *feral*. After class I made a beeline for the dictionary. The definition read, "having reverted to the wild state as from domestication: *a pack of feral dogs roaming the woods.*"

I could not fathom *feral*. What conditions might precede such a reversion? Was *feral* a regression, then? A falling from grace? Or, might *feral* be closer to a return, a reawakening to a truth always known but long forgotten? Afraid of being singled out in class and self-conscious about what I deemed my rudimentary vocabulary, I recited the dictionary definition aloud to myself over and over again. No matter how hard I pressed that definition into my mind, it would not stick. I kept forgetting what *feral* meant, as if its definition were a foreign substance my mind could not—or would not—as-similate. I was unaware then that true meaning cannot be imposed on the mind. That nuanced understanding arrives through the body and registers—sometimes with a shudder—deep in the chest.

One of the stories I wrote for "Professor Tweed's" class was about an adolescent girl with anorexia. He sat at a long table at the front of the room, picked up my story, flapped its pages in the air and said to the class, "I don't hear a voice. Do you hear a voice?" Silence. A fist in my throat. "You can have all the energy of Tolstoy," he con-tinued, "but if you don't have a voice?" I wish I had said something, then, in my defense. But I was years from knowing that a voice, like a self, can retreat into hiding and that sometimes, in order to hear it, you have to listen for the deeper story it has been conditioned not to tell...the story that so many men like Professor Tweed have been conditioned not to hear. With a flip of his wrist, he tossed my story aside. It landed on the table with a shudder.

Forward to the fall of 1992.

I sat clutching my composition notebook as the circle of desks filled with women my mother's age, women who'd raged their way through the sixties, the decade in which I was born. A petite white woman with hands so pale they looked translucent wrote on the chalkboard *Writing Re-creatively: A Spiritual Quest for Women. Gail Ranadive.* Her voice was soft, like mine, but her tone? Indomitable. "We are not creating something out of nothing," she said. "Rather, we will write in order to tap into what's already within us, hidden, hibernating, waiting to be reawakened and given voice."

She'd created this course for women, she explained, because she'd noticed a pattern in her workshops. When it happened that women were the only ones in attendance because the men were, by some fluke, all absent at the same time, the women's writing took an unexpected turn: raw, wild, untamed.

Feral.

Together we would write from prompts designed to help us "recreate the images, symbols, and metaphors of our own lives, as women." We would read our writing aloud, and though we were free to pass, she encouraged us not to. "Each person has a piece of our collective story," she said. "You will each hear yourself and others name what you didn't know you knew."

I may have been the youngest by a generation, but I knew what she was talking about. A year earlier, in October 1991, I watched Anita Hill speak her truth before a stone-faced Judiciary Committee, and I found myself crying silent tears as she named what I didn't know I knew. When she said, in her defense, that she could not explain why she hadn't spoken before now, recognition shuddered in my chest.

The Judiciary Committee—almost exclusively white men dressed, let's say, in tweed jackets—sat at a long table at the front of the chamber. One by one they flapped the pages of Anita Hill's testimony. When one of the men tossed her testimony aside with a flip of his wrist, a fist rose in my throat.

I don't hear a voice. Do you hear a voice?

After her testimony, I sat at my pie hutch where untold women before me had kneaded dough and, perhaps, cried silent tears, and I wrote in my notebook *Anita Hill.* Then I wrote *I, too, have been sexually harassed.* Then I wrote *Has every woman been sexually harassed?* It would be months before the term *date rape* would bleed from my pen, years—and dozens of notebooks later—before I would realize that the story I'd once written about a girl with anorexia carried a deeper truth that had, for a time, awakened me, sobbing, in the dead of night.

"I challenge you to name your own truth," Gail Ranadive said.

Week after week I wrote with that circle of women. One by one we read our words aloud. The more I came to know the nuance of each woman's voice, its longings, leaps, and shivers, the less separate our voices sounded. Not that they became one and the same. They did not. But I began to hear what I can only describe as a collective reckoning. It started low, a rumble in the chest, then shed its inhibitions as voice by voice it chorused into an unbridled howl.

When "Writing Re-Creatively" ended, I wrote a thank-you letter to Gail and my writing circle. "Each of you taught me to howl," I wrote, and on the word *howl,* as if on cue, a pack of dogs began to howl in the distance. The howl started low but soon harmonized into a chorus howl that registered in my chest so keenly I wondered if I myself was howling. No. It was the dogs, not me. But I understood then that I, too, was part of a pack—Anita Hill, Gail Ranadive, the women in my writing circle, the women who'd bent over this pie hutch before me—and that together we had, voice by voice, reverted to the wild state as from domestication. *Feral.* The pie hutch shuddered.

MARILYN BOUSQUIN is the founder of Writing Women's Lives™, where she teaches women who are done with silence how to free their voice, claim their truth, and write their memoir stories with confidence, craft, and consciousness. Her book reviews and memoir essays appear in *River Teeth, Literary Mama, Under the Gum Tree, Superstition Review,* and *Pithead Chapel,* and her essay "Against Memory" was a finalist for AROHO's Orlando Prize for Creative Nonfiction. Her memoir-in-progress explores the correlation between the female body, self, and voice. A broadside of Lucille Clifton's poem "won't you celebrate with me" hangs above her writing table, which is painted robin's-egg blue. Find out more at www.writingwomenslives.com.

HALE BRADT

on Wilber Bradt

My father knew it was a historic time when, in the fall of 1940, his National Guard division was notified that it would be inducted into federal service early in 1941. The US was not yet in the war—the Japanese attack on Pearl Harbor in Hawaii would take place in December 1941—but most of continental Europe was already under the boots of the Axis powers. At 40, my father, Wilber, was a chemistry professor at the University of Maine in Orono. He had long been a guardsman, first in his home state of Indiana, later in Washington State where he held his first teaching job and met Norma— later to become his wife and my mother—and now in Maine. Because of those transfers, he was under rank for his age—only a captain. He was also way overweight, 240 pounds at an even six feet. As such, he was not qualified for active duty.

But he had trained for war for over 20 years in the Guard and was determined to serve his country when it called. On a crash diet he brought his weight down to 190 pounds, and thus was able to enter the service with his Maine field artillery regiment. After 19 months in training camps in Florida and Mississippi, his division was shipped to the South Pacific to help arrest the Japanese advance threatening Australia. He would not see his home country again for a full three years.

He fought in the Solomon Islands, where he was wounded twice; in New Guinea; and in the Philippines, where he was three times awarded the Silver Star medal for personal heroism. He was commander of a field artillery battalion in these actions and was prepared to lead a regimental combat team of 4,500 men in the invasion of Japan had the war continued. He did not expect to survive that likely bloodbath. But he did survive the war, only to commit suicide six weeks after his return home. The reasons, I would come to learn, were complex. The transition to civilian life was much more difficult for him than we realized at the time, as was the challenge of forgetting war and all of its horrors. I was one week shy of my 15th birthday on the day he died.

It was not until decades later, on my 50th birthday, that I was prompted by a conversation with a sister to see if I might have any of the letters I knew my dad had written home during his long absence. In a basement file cabinet I found an envelope of about a dozen he had written me. At some point, my mother had sent them to me, and I had filed and forgotten them. As I read them that evening, I was struck by how literate and beautifully descriptive they were. His fatherly advice to his young son, and his descriptions of Army life in camps and in combat, were vivid and insightful.

He had written prolifically during his more than four years in the Army. Now I realized that his letters would be a new window not only into the Pacific War, but also into his life, psyche, and evolving relationship with my mother. Over the next few years, I explored his story with great energy. I searched for and located some 700 of his letters, mostly written to his wife (my mother) and his parents; interviewed family members and his military colleagues, many of whom were still living in the early 1980s; visited the Pacific battle sites where he fought; and scoured archives for documents and photographs.

I knew that I was the only person who could put the letters into context and fill out the complexities of my parents' lives; some of the letters are quite personal and are not easily shared, even today. This task added a new dimension to my life and led me in directions very different from the astrophysics of my "day job." It involved me in new dialogues: with my own sisters, with a Japanese colonel who fought opposite my dad, and later with a book editor, designer, and printer. In 2015, at age 84, I finally finished putting Wilber's letters, together with background context, into publishable form. I hope that the completed trilogy—*Wilber's War: An American Family's Journey through World War II*—does justice to his story and to our understanding of the profound way that war shapes our lives.

My dad wrote of his love for Norma ever so poetically, of his surroundings with vivid descriptions, and of his fellow soldiers with admiration and humor. He wrote movingly about combat, the loss of friends, and his concerns about Norma's well-being, and he noted his own moods with insight. But he also did his best to be father and mentor to his son and daughter. For example, he wrote to me the night before he would be shipped out overseas, when I was 11 years old:

Sept. 30, 1942. Hello Big Son— This is just a note to
tell you that it is a good day here. Tomorrow is the
first of October. If I were home we'd plan a camping
trip for next weekend. How about Mt. Katahdin?
　　I want you to be my Liaison Officer in the
family. A Ln. O. helps keep contact between two
commanding officers—Norma and Wilber. He
is responsible for sending messages about how
things are going at the other headquarters. You
can consider that I am at the forward HQ and you
are at the Main HQ. —I love you Hale. Wilber.

He was giving me leave to take on some responsibility for the
family at home. And 18 months later, he wrote this from New Zealand
after hearing from my mother that I had been to a dance with a girl.

April 3, 1944. Dear Hale— This sex business is pretty
powerful stuff when you get a little older and can give
you either a lot of fun or a lot of trouble....I know
now that it is wrong to do anything that would harm
either the body or spirit or reputation of another
person. Doing anything, which a girl or you would
look back on as being cheap or that would make
either of you ashamed afterward, would be wrong....
it is therefore up to us men to see that our girls don't
feel sorry for anything the next day or month.

These letters and the many others he wrote guided my actions
in those vulnerable years. But above all, it was his realization of the
historical importance of his wartime experiences and the willingness
to record them in intimate detail that inspired me to flesh out this
rich story of a soldier, a couple and a family caught up in wartime.

When I was young, his example helped me become the person I am; later, that example turned me into a historian and biographer. In exploring his letters and life, I met him for a second time, this time with the perspective of an adult rather than a child. His mentorship, by example, is still is at work in me, more than 70 years after his death.

HALE BRADT is a published author and retired physics professor who served on the faculty of the Massachusetts Institute of Technology from 1961 to 2001. During the Korean conflict, he served in the US Navy. He shares his parents' stories with insight, compassion, and a wealth of photos, documents, and records that bring their collective experience to life in *Wilber's War: An American Family's Journey Through World War II*, which is available in two editions: the trilogy, published as a boxed set, and the one-volume condensation, *Wilber's War (abridged)*. Find out more at www.wilberswar.com.

BARBARA ALANA BROOKS

on Jamie Gail Brooks Beck

As the precious pink bundle was placed into my arms, my stomach fluttered with nervous excitement. Who was this soul coming into our lives? My husband Bud and four-year-old son, Steven, had traveled with me to pick up this tiny new person who was destined to become a permanent part of our family. My dream to have a daughter in my life was coming true. I remember that she and I looked into each other's eyes with curiosity and fascination.

We named her Jamie Gail. She truly was a gale—in the way she arrived and the way she lived her life. A tempest and even, sometimes, a hurricane, she dashed through her childhood. She looked like a small angel with her blonde, wavy hair but she was gloriously human, racing around like a jet, bumping into furniture, spilling her drinks and being generally mischievous. Her limbs were always bruised from crashing into things. (In today's world with child abuse in the public eye, we might have been put in jail!) Her voice was as strong and energetic as the rest of her, instantly claiming our attention.

From day one, we recognized a very quick mind along with her speedy body. In grade school she was tested for the gifted program and passed with flying colors, although she didn't like being in a special class. In high school she managed to graduate with honors. I have no idea how, since she skipped most of her senior year and they told her she had to make up the time in detention in order to graduate! A picture of Jamie graduating from high school captures her personality perfectly. *Here I am! Made it through,* it seems to proclaim. Everyone in the picture looks serious except Jamie. Her energy says, *This is all pretty ridiculous.*

Jamie grew up tall and beautiful. Her voice was commanding and her presence powerful. When she walked into a room, you had to perk up and take notice. She wasn't ready to settle down in college, so she dropped out in the middle of her freshman year, moving to Colorado to be near Steven. Over and over I was reminded of Jamie's passion for life and her authenticity. Right or wrong, she was hard to argue with. You couldn't stop her from being her. We did try a little, but eventually gave up. It was a lesson in accepting others for who they were—not an easy task for parents!

Since we had adopted Jamie, we had limited access to information on her background. She never showed interest in searching for her biological relatives, although I did encourage her at one point. Naturally I wondered how she felt about it, and was delighted that it never seemed to matter to her. I know it didn't matter to us. One of her friends wrote to me, saying, "Through our many talks about life, conception, actually having babies and so on…adoption came up frequently—no matter what the point of our conversation was she always, always made it clear that she never felt that she was adopted. You were her family, no matter blood, DNA, or anything else. I can remember her vividly saying 'they are me and I am them.'" I love that her friend shared those words, which ring like a beautiful chime inside me.

As she matured, Jamie transformed into a magical, amazing adult who was smart, organized, funny, and full of laughter as well as a sharp tongue and quick wit. When she wed Devin, the man of her dreams, they created Chloe and Wyatt and made a happy home together. Now that she had her own kids, she took some of the things she had scoffed at earlier much more seriously.

Jamie and I became very close after she married and had children of her own. I felt like she really understood me to a "T," and that was so remarkable and lovely. I never had to explain myself to her. She got it over the years. As far as my understanding her, well, not as much. Deeply as I loved her, she remained in many ways a wonderful enigma.

Jamie died suddenly from an aneurysm in 2015, at the age of 38. Her death devastated all of us, especially her husband and young children. Shattering loss seems to stop the world and turns it black and white. Abruptly my world went from brilliant color to a drab gray. I looked around but I really could not feel anything. Slowly, my eyes and my heart are experiencing more color again. Loss is everywhere but so is life. The world is so much more beautiful when you really know, beyond lip service or clichés, that this is all temporary.

I will miss Jamie's vivacious presence in my life for the rest of my days. I'm also grateful for all that I've learned from her. She was the most genuine person I have ever been with. There was never a doubt who she was, where you stood with her or what she thought. Without manipulation or pretense she was just herself, tough as nails at some times, soft as silk at others, loving and authentic always. As Jamie, our dancing tempest, twirled and spun, breezed and gusted through her days on earth with boundless energy and then left us just as decisively, her example has helped teach me how to be myself, without any masks. That is her greatest lesson.

———————————————

BARBARA ALANA BROOKS attended the University of Wisconsin and graduated from American University in Washington D.C. with a degree in elementary education. Barb's journey as a teacher, mom, wife, traveler and adventurer, along with her lifelong path of searching and exploration, have all enriched her life as an artist and writer. Her books include *Expressions of Spirit*, which depicts the richly soulful mandala art Barb has created over many years, and *The Coloring Journal: An Awakening Journey Through the Art of Barbara Alana Brooks*, which offers images of the mandalas to color coupled with additional tools for reflection and clarity. Barb lives in Florida with her husband Bud. Find out more at www.barbsartwork.com.

ROBIN LYNN BROOKS

on AnDréya Wilde

I sit in the corner of the kitchen in an armchair. I am tense, as curled up into myself as I can be, my feet tucked tight beneath me.

My voice shakes as I whisper into the phone to my therapist so that I cannot be heard. It is hard to speak what I feel, the words coming broken and slow. I was silenced as a child and do not know, still, how to reach inside and speak what is there. But, gradually, it begins to come.

I knew little of who I was or what my needs were, when I was a child. I did not know that we all deserve kindness. I knew no kindness; I was not allowed needs, nor even to exist.

From an early age, as much as I was able, I became what my parents wanted me to be, in the hope they would not hurt me. They taught me I was bad, worthless, and to blame for all that had been done. I felt I deserved whatever happened.

These feelings transported themselves throughout my life into every relationship. I drew abuse to me, feeling I deserved nothing better.

My childhood stripped me of the ability to trust. How could I trust anyone when the two people who were supposed to love and care for me abused me?

Ashamed of who I was, I hid behind a mask. Unable to trust anyone, I lived in a perpetual state of fear, of hypervigilance, waiting "like a soldier in the jungle not knowing when a bullet would hit," as I later wrote in my poem "No Boundaries."

Because the abuse was more than my child self could withstand, I left my body. I dissociated. I have few memories of my childhood and came away with only one conscious memory of the abuse—when I said "No" to my father when I was 17. With acute PTSD, I continued to live separate from my body, so much so that when I touched the grass, my fingers could not feel it.

> My heart moves
> to the sound
> of tears not fallen,
> waiting for the emptiness
> to find its river out.

This was who I was at 47, when I met Dr. AnDréya Wilde—Dréya.

Spirit brought us together. My twin sister, also a therapist, gave me Dréya's name. I saw her first when she had an office in Brattleboro, Vermont.

I remember standing at the end of a hall, at a tall window under the peak of a low, slanted ceiling. I was looking out at the lush land-scape of an abundant vegetable garden below and the low green mountains of New England beyond, and I was nervous. I did not know what to expect.

We had spoken on the phone once, so, from behind me, I recognized Dréya's rich and vibrant voice calling me in. Then, within a room colored in deep crimson and gold—near as dark as a womb—first I sat on the edge of and then felt comfortable enough to lie down on the plush, ruby couch. She drew me out, and as I witnessed her ability to "see" and "know" my mother and others as I spoke of them, warm feelings toward her soon quickened.

I began seeing Dréya regularly at what became her office in Hatfield, Massachusetts, near the Smith College town of Northampton.

In the weeks that followed, then months and then years, Dréya joined me on every journey no matter how elusive, how wrought from my subconscious or my spirit. As she sat in the nest of her deeply cushioned armchair, an incarnation of a cross between Buddha and the Great Mother, she cajoled and challenged me. She held me as a newborn to her voluminous, metaphorical breast. She let me know that she was there for me.

Almost immediately, as we worked together, through past life regression, trance work, and traditional therapy, more memories surfaced. When my mother died in 2009—my second parent to die—my body and psyche must have felt it safe enough because the worst memories began to come.

Dréya helped me through each step of the way, acting as therapist, friend, peer, mother, and mentor. Through her I took my first baby steps towards trusting another person. I experienced what it was to be loved unconditionally. With her I learned to access and express anger, until then nearly impossible for me. She held me emotionally as I reached the deepest abyss, and she lit the way for me as I found my way out.

Over the period of five years after my mother died and the worst memories surfaced, after not writing poetry for over 20 years, poems began to come. Along with therapy, in writing these poems I began to unearth who I really was, and I found my voice. I read Dréya every poem, and many times, after a memory came, she encouraged me to write another, to reach deeper, explore, and transform what had happened to me.

These worst memories left me broken and in severe pain. It became difficult for me to be out in public and difficult to work. Afterwards, I was a different person, as I had now lived—really for the first time—all that had been done to me.

Slowly, with Dréya's help, I built a sense of my own self-worth. I learned that I am good, that I have value, and that I deserve to be treated with honor and respect.

I came out of isolation, discovering my local women's center where I began writing with other trauma survivors, a group of whom I still write with weekly. When these women shared with me that what I wrote was helping them, I decided to make my poems into a book.

Dréya organized these hundreds of poems into chapters that follow the natural order of healing. A survivor can read the poems sequentially or choose a chapter that resonates with her in the moment and know she is not alone. Demonstrated throughout are the healing tools that I used, along with messages of hope, validation, strength, courage, and inspiration. The finished book is called *The Blooming of the Lotus*.

Dréya encouraged me to "tell" my story through my book to public audiences, and I have, many times. I now also lead healing workshops for women when I can.

I continue to write healing books for survivors and have now also published *The Blooming of the Lotus for Professionals*. Two other books are written and awaiting publishing. I am working on a few others.

When I think back to that woman curled up tight in her chair, whispering and shaking, and then I look to who I have become, it feels like a miracle.

I no longer live behind a mask but at the edge of my skin, fully present and alive.

I know what situations are good for me, and, as much as possible, I stay away from those that are not. I recognize it is my birthright to be treated with kindness and respect in relationship, and I will never again allow into my life those who would hurt me.

I have found the strength that was already inside me, and I have discovered and now recognize the beauty of my being. Directly because of Dréya's mentoring of me, I have come to understand, too, that it is my honor and soul's purpose to give back and share with others what I have been given. It is my utmost desire to help others in whatever way I can so they might find their own way to healing and to the fulfillment of who they are.

Now, I do not only allow myself to exist. So much more, I am learning how to live and breathe my greatest self as I become who I was born to be. I would not be here today without the extreme capability, guidance, love, and support of my amazing mentor, Dr. AnDréya Wilde.

…Such a gift
to be here
in this life
at this time
with who
I have become

ROBIN LYNN BROOKS is a published poet and playwright whose art has traveled nationwide. She has an M.F.A. in Sculpture from the School of the Museum of Fine Arts in Boston. Her last body of work, *Earth Mothers*, is a series of life-size and larger women made of earth. She is also a book designer. The author of the poetic memoir *The Blooming of the Lotus: a spiritual journey from trauma into light*, Robin writes healing books, speaks, and leads workshops for women survivors. Robin lives in western Massachusetts on an old farm that borders the state forest. It was here that she found her first mothering—in the earth. The white pines behind her house shelter her. The lake in the woods is her temple. This was the place of nurturance that gave her the support to heal. Robin's website is www.bloomingofthelotus.com.

GRAYSON CHESSER

on Miles Hancock

Virginia's Eastern Shore, where my family have lived since the 1600s, is a narrow peninsula bounded by the Atlantic Ocean on the east and the Chesapeake Bay on the west, with a group of barrier islands along its eastern edge. Geographically isolated for most of its history, it's a place that has its own distinct character and traditions. My family have always been farmers, hunters, and watermen. I feel fortunate to be able to live in the same place and in much the same way as my family have always lived, and to do what I wanted to do in life. Those are luxuries not many people today enjoy.

I've been making wooden duck decoys for nearly six decades now, and it's never lost its fascination. It wasn't looked on as an art form when I began, and thinking you could make a living doing it was about as practical as thinking you could be Mickey Mantle. But decoy-making had flourished on the Eastern Shore because decoys were necessity for waterfowl hunting. Nathan Cobb, Jr., "Umbrella" Watson, Ira Hudson, Doug Jester, the Ward brothers, "Cigar" Daisy, and Miles Hancock, among others: many earlier decoy carvers, as well as those still working when I was young, are now regarded as folk artists. The prices their decoys command would amaze them.

Becoming a decoy carver wasn't something that interested most kids I knew. But all I ever wanted was to be a decoy carver and hunting guide. I liked art, loved exploring the seaside marshes, and was fascinated by waterfowl. It seemed natural to begin to create decoys myself, and then to seek the help I needed to do it better.

There was just one book on decoys that I remember from those days—a guide to decoy making by Eugene V. Connett. Today, you can learn decoy-making from books, classes, and videos. There's nothing wrong with that—my techniques are the subject of a book and I've enjoyed teaching classes as well as mentoring decoy artists through the Virginia Folklife Program. But there's something richer and deeper in a personal, one-on-one connection that lasts over time—a chance to learn from someone's example and character, as well as from their techniques.

Most men begin carving in their late teens or early twenties, but the men of my father's generation spent those years in World War II. For the most part, the decoy carvers I learned from were of my grandfather's generation. Though I got help and advice from Lloyd Tyler, the Ward brothers and "Cigar" Daisy—all legends—it was Miles Hancock who was my most important teacher. I first met him in 1962, when I was in my early teens. In his 70s by that time, he lived on Chincoteague Island, about twelve miles or so from my home. The day my mom drove me over to his place the first time, I brought along a pair of the decoys I had made. They were teal, really ugly, as square as shoeboxes and just plain bad. Mr. Hancock just looked at them and told me that I had a real nice paint job but needed to round them up. It wasn't the first time he had been kind to a younger person and it wouldn't be the last.

I always liked to paint and had trouble with carving, something that Mr. Hancock helped me improve. The basic design of my own decoys is not dissimilar to his. He was one of the first carvers on the Shore who made their decoys with a really wide flat bottom, a characteristic that makes them more stable in the water than are the sleeker, more rounded shapes. Miles Hancock's decoys aren't all great pieces of art, but they're all great decoys. I appreciate being able to make part of my living selling my work to collectors and having it looked on as art. But it's the tradition of the working decoy that I most value, and I design most of my decoys with use in mind. I still work as a waterfowl guide, and what I really love is seeing a rig of decoys I've made out there on the water.

Mr. Hancock had a medium-sized build and snow white hair. He probably shaved about once a week and usually wore clothes that were splattered with paint. He didn't change into something fancier when well-off or important people showed up at his workshop, as they did over the years. He was an unpretentious man who felt no need to impress. I remember his wife, who I called Miss Bertha and who I also loved, fussing. "I can't believe you were out there dressed like that," she would say.

I probably visited him once every week or two weeks while I was a teenager. I'd take the decoys I had made to show him, and he was never too busy to spend time with me. Rather than telling me specifically what to do, he'd suggest trying this or fixing that. I remember seeing this old black decoy on a shelf in his workshop. I told Mr.

Hancock that I thought it was the prettiest one I'd ever seen. He told me that it was by Umbrella Watson, another Chincoteague islander. That was my first introduction to Watson's work, which has taught me a lot about painting over the years. I feel lucky that I have been able to learn so much from collecting and looking at older decoys.

I soaked up the way Miles Hancock carved, painted and finished his decoys, as well as everything he said when he stopped to talk. Growing up on the Eastern Shore you learned most of what you knew from the oral tradition, not school. You'd learn all about your great-great grandpas, what their likes and dislikes were, how they lived. My family is full of tremendous storytellers and Mr. Hancock was a great storyteller too. Over the years I got to know something of his life. His mother had died when he was a young boy and his father didn't have the means to raise him and his siblings, so he was raised by an older couple. He went to school for only a couple of years—I remember him telling me that he had learned to count playing marbles. He had to start making his living young. He began as a market hunter and, after federal legislation put a stop to that, became a guide and decoy carver.

Miles Hancock taught me a lot about decoys, but even more about living. He helped shape my understanding of success and what it was to be a good man. Mr. Hancock didn't have a lot of money, but on the terms he cared about he was very successful. He had a good marriage. He could do what he wanted to do. He was well respected and he respected others in turn. He was a very humble man. The only thing I ever remember him being proud about was his ability as a hunter—he was regarded as the best shot on Chincoteague, despite having one bad eye. He was a member of Union Baptist Church, but he was never the kind of man who preached to you. His life was his testimony.

I made up my mind pretty early on that if I could help anyone keep the tradition of carving alive, I'd gladly pass on what I knew. Artists sometimes talk about secret tricks or techniques, but I don't want to carry any knowledge to the grave with me. If I do, it will all have been wasted. Miles Hancock and other "old masters" of decoy carving not only shared their secrets, they taught me for free. I can't equal the gifts they gave me, but I try to repay them by passing on what they taught me. The same goes for preserving the environment and the way of life of the Eastern Shore.

I've been fortunate enough to receive a lot of recognition in my life. One of the honors that means the most is that Miles Hancock thought enough of me that I was chosen as one of the pallbearers at his funeral. He died in 1974, but I still think of him often. The best way I can sum him up is to say that you might be able to find a better carver than Miles Hancock, but you couldn't find a better man.

GRAYSON CHESSER is a waterfowling guide, conservationist, and decoy maker whose work, highly sought out by collectors, has been exhibited at the Smithsonian Institution and Cummer Museum among other venues. *Making Decoys: The Century-Old Way,* which Chesser co-authored with Curtis J. Badger, shares his decoy-making techniques as well as the carving traditions of Virginia's Eastern Shore. He and his wife Dawn own and operate the Holden Creek Gun Club in Sanford, Virginia. Grayson Chesser has given back to the life of the Eastern Shore in a variety of ways: through his service as a game warden, his tenure on the Board of Supervisors of Accomack County, and his participation as a mentor/teacher in the Virginia Folklife Apprenticeship Program, which honored him as a Virginia Folk Master in 2004.

MARY EDWARDS

on John Luther Adams

I have been fortunate enough to have a variety of mentors, teachers, collaborators, and what might be called cultural godmothers and godfathers, all of whom have informed and inspired my work in music over the years. Paradoxically, a few of the most influential mentors I have had are the ones I haven't known well if at all. But the sense of direction, permission or possibility these "distant mentors" offer can be profound. My connection to the person I chose to write about here, the contemporary American composer John Luther Adams, exemplifies the way even someone who we don't know or interact with personally can still transform not just the actual work we produce but the way we think about that work, our process and our world.

A theme that has run through my music from the beginning, becoming more central over the years, is the idea of immersive sound experiences: sound as an enveloping temporal, spatial, even architectural form. Some 12 or 15 years ago I was working with academic mentors who encouraged me to think outside the box in terms of genre and what I wanted to do with my music. I remember one of those mentors, the composer Laura Koplewitz, saying something like "Okay. You're writing these pieces about airports. You're writing these pieces about woodland experiences. Have you considered sound installation?"

In response, I began to investigate artists working with sound installation and other intermedia forms, John Luther Adams among them. I learned about Adams before he won Pulitzer and Grammy awards and also before it was possible to find and hear most pieces of music with a digital click. He had a respected name among contemporary composers but his work was something you had to seek. I sought out and listened to his music and gradually learned more about him and his career. His story, sensibility, and music resonated deeply with me.

Like me, Adams is originally from the New York area and has what in some senses is a typical musical background: he wrote music, he performed, he taught music. But his career has also been transformatively shaped by his passion for environmental causes, particularly after he moved to Alaska, where he lived for decades until a few years ago. Interviews discuss the moment in his life when he felt that he had to choose between focusing on environmental change and focusing on music, both of which are consuming careers. He felt that he could best serve through his music—an intuition that has certainly proved true. His music is profoundly influenced by the natural world, the threats to the planet, and what he's called "that region between place and culture…between environment and imagination."

Among other things, my exploration of his work affirmed the possibilities inherent in my own fascination with place and my interest in forms including aleatoric music. In the Western canon, we expect to hear a piece of music that has a beginning, middle and end and that is performed in largely the same way each time. Aleatoric music works differently—Werner Meyer-Eppler, who coined the term, said that it involves a course of sound events that is "determined in general but depends on chance in detail." "Noises" considered distractions in the performance of a piece of traditional music become part of the experience in work that's not meant to be performed in a concert hall. The assumptions about how we should hear things and what we think we know are challenged, and our inextricable and often complex connection to a particular place is affirmed. We are not so much listening to a pre-existing work but going on a journey to new and deeper levels of ourselves. All of this and more moved and inspired me as I explored Adams's work.

Many of these thoughts and threads came together when Kathleen Hancock, director of the Grimshaw-Gudewicz Art Gallery in Massachusetts, commissioned me to create a composition and sound installation a few years ago. I have always been interested in geography and bodies of water and I knew that I wanted to do something specific to this particular place. The piece I created took as its starting point the Quequechan River, one of the network of waterways of the Fall River area, where the gallery is located. At one time crucial drivers of the region's industry and commerce, rivers like the Quequechan were later depleted, polluted, and made invisible in many senses of the word. Now people are interested in bringing back the Quequechan and other rivers like it.

For my piece I researched the history of both the area and the river. In addition, for almost six months I visited the river one weekend a month and recorded different points in its course. Not all of the Quequechan is accessible—a significant stretch of it has been covered up by I-95. But enough of it could be experienced for my purposes. In one early visit in January 2013, I recorded the ice breaking up and melting, the sluggish movement of the water. I recorded the more rapid, flowing motion of the water as the seasons changed and also recorded at the Fall River cascades, around which some of the old industrial mills and warehouses still stand.

In my studio, I used an audio program to weave the recordings together into a 14-minute piece. Orchestrated with a series of musical motifs, it creates the sound illusion of traveling the length of the river, going through its different parts and its different points. I juxtaposed vocal sounds with and into that, haunting voices that suggested those (both old and young) who worked at the area's mills in their heyday. I wasn't interested in being literal or in making an explicit political statement of any kind. I wanted to capture the sense of the memories the water still carries, its characteristic "speech," and its complex environmental relationship with the human communities through which it runs.

My piece, which I entitled *per/severance,* was installed in the gallery in tandem with a work called *This Bright Morning* by the visual artist Charlotte Hamlin. You could stand under the mysterious, evocative root shapes she suspended from the ceiling and hear, in my piece, the sounds of the river. During the opening at which *per/severance* premiered, a woman whose family had lived in the area for many generations, and who had found out that I was the composer and sound artist, came up to me. She threw her arms around me, crying. She said, "Thank you for giving the river a voice."

It was such a lovely moment, and one that reinforced my sense of creative direction. Built around three very different settings, my most recent work, *The Space Between: A Sound Trilogy,* uses sound to investigate the tensions between essence and impermanence, desire and uncertainty, nature and architecture, and absence and presence. The sense of possibility that listening to John Luther Adams has given me, and the example of the way he builds on elements of chance and place, are very much part of what inspires and underlies this trilogy as well as the other pieces emerging for me now.

I was fortunate enough to attend the New York City premiere of Adams's work *Become Ocean,* which went on to win the 2014 Pulitzer Prize for Music, and to meet him briefly at that time. About a month later, I attended a music conference in North Carolina. There I was invited to participate in a 40-person percussion outfit performing one of John Luther Adams's pieces outdoors on the campus of the University of North Carolina in Asheville. Adams the person was not present, but Adams the thinker, composer and environmentalist was very much felt and appreciated. For me, the chance to help perform a composition by this mentor who has been so important to me—to inhabit it, as it were, from the inside—was a moving and unforgettable experience.

MARY EDWARDS is a composer, songwriter and sound designer whose projects range from recordings and performances "evocative of epic cinematic soundtracks combined with lyrical intimacy" (*Time Out* Magazine) to immersive environmental and architectural sound installations. Themes of temporality, impermanence, nostalgia, longing, childhood and the natural world are interspersed throughout her work. She has worked as performer or composer on a wide variety of film, theatre and television scores (BBC, PBS, The Learning Channel and ABC-TV); is a practitioner of the sound healing arts; and has lectured widely as a composer-in-residence on acoustic ecology, which studies music and the relationship between living beings and their environment, mediated through sound. Find out more about Mary's work at www.maryedwardsmusic.com.

KATHY EVANS

on Ronald Breitfelder

'm not a mathematician and I never especially liked the subject, except for the three years I spent in Mr. Breitfelder's honors math class. I mention that it was honors not to impress, but because that made a difference. It's why I had him for three years instead of just one; he was the main honors math teacher at my high school. It's why the same kids were in his class year after year, a quirky collection of nerds like Chuck, brainy bad boys like Scott, and Ruth, who made her note cards out of cut-up cereal boxes, who liked to laugh, and who wore dirndl dresses with laced-up vests to school. Her parents were German immigrants. We had some loners, a smattering of popular, good-looking types, a set of twins, and the whole of Latin Club.

We regarded one another with a palpable mutual respect. There was gentle teasing, spirited debate, and a genuine interest in the subject, thanks to our beloved Mr. Breitfelder. His class, as well as Mr. Breitfelder himself, was a refuge for us. Here you could relax, you could feel less miserable than usual, and you could revel in the oft-hidden glories of learning.

Mr. Breitfelder was only ten years older than we were, with dark hair, long sideburns, bright dark eyes, and rough, handsome good looks. He was also the football coach, and he and his petite and smiling wife chaperoned the dances. He loved math and his math students, and he made the same dumb jokes day after day: "Suppose we study velocity today. I need a volunteer, someone I can hold out the window. Mr. Melman?"

He called us all "Mr." and "Miss" and expected the best we had to give. Once during a test I accidentally saw somebody else's paper—it really was an accident—and seeing it made me immediately realize my error on a geometry proof. I wrote Mr. Breitfelder a long note on the back of my paper about how I had not intended to cheat but after I glimpsed the key part of the problem, I couldn't un-see it and so I wrote the proof correctly, but would not have had I not seen it, so he could take off the points if he wanted and I was so sorry, and my note was even more rambling than this sentence. He called me in after class the next day and sat on the edge of his desk as he always did, while I sat in the first desk in the row. He was no pushover, but we talked through the proof and the problem, and seeing that I knew the material, he decided that he would give me full credit. He said, "I know you weren't trying to cheat and I'll know you'll be careful to keep your eyes on your own paper in the future." I would. I would do anything for Mr. Breitfelder's respect, which shone in those bright dark eyes.

We received an assignment to write a paper on any topic we

wished related to mathematics. Our instructions were just to clear it with him and go to town (figuratively speaking). I chose the life of Archimedes, Mr. Give-Me-a-Lever-and-a-Place-to-Stand-and-I-Will-Move-the-Earth. Archimedes was also Mr. Eureka, which is what he shouted while running through the streets naked (he had been bathing at the time) when he discovered the principle that the displacement of water can determine the volume of an irregularly shaped object—in this case, a votive crown belonging to the king. He was able to tell the king whether his crown was made of pure gold (it wasn't) or whether in fact the crown-maker was a shyster (he was). These things are with me 45 years later because I learned them, well, out of love for Mr. Breitfelder.

My brilliant friend Vicki and I were Mr. Breitfelder's "lab assistants," an official-sounding title I liked. For two and a half of our three years with Mr. Breitfelder, Vicki and I spent our free hour in a tiny windowless room off his classroom, grading papers or stapling tests together. Sometimes there were no papers to grade. Then Vicki and I talked about life, and not just boys—she is now a professor of Chinese religion and philosophy, if that gives you an idea. When his students were quietly occupied, Mr. Breitfelder might join us for a few minutes to see if we'd solved all the world's problems yet. We hadn't, but with Mr. Breitfelder around, we weren't so afraid of them.

And so it was that I confided my weekend activities to Vicki during that free hour and she began to worry about my double life. Good girl during the week, I sought out my hood friends when the weekend rolled around, tough boys who hung around smoking behind Coney Chef, who rolled up their cigarette packs in their shirtsleeves, whose hair hung low over their eyes, who skipped class whenever they felt like it, who were going nowhere fast, wearing black leather. Among their ranks was the brainy bad boy Scott, who would that summer become my boyfriend. One morning he drank ten beers before the start of school and threw up in the hall outside Mr. Breitfelder's classroom. Mr. Breitfelder went out to deal with him and was gone a long time. Scott would one day hold a Ph.D. in microbiology, and it was Mr. Breitfelder who saved him from his life of crime. Of that I'm sure.

With the hoods I smoked pot, drank Schlitz and Hudepohl (that's another beer, for you non-Midwesterners) by the quart, and rode in the back of somebody's Camaro while the guys stole street signs, construction cones, and, once, eight-track tape decks.

It was a wild time. I thought I had it all under control, but I was skating close to the edge. Vicki, a straight arrow, could see the danger and brought Mr. Breitfelder onto the scene. Again he asked me to stay after class. He leaned on his desk and asked how things were at home (not good), how I was spending my free time (I confessed, because it was a sweet relief and I could tell he already knew), and if anything was worrying me. Sitting in the first desk in the row, I broke down in tears. Not so much because I was coming apart at the seams—I was, though it was too soon for me to tell—but because I had so disappointed Mr. Breitfelder, or at least made him worry about my future, if not my soul. He didn't smile, he didn't frown, he held my gaze. Saying very little, he bestowed kindness and compassion along with the expectation that I would do better going forward.

The fog cleared. I made some promises and I meant them, though I'd lose my way many more times traversing the tricky years of adolescence and young adulthood. More importantly, I walked out of there feeling Mr. Breitfelder's presence in my life, his strength, and his loving willingness to face things with me as they came, mathematical and otherwise.

Unlike the king's crown, Mr. Breitfelder was pure gold.

Personal historian **KATHY EVANS** has been asking people to tell their stories to her since she was a child and writing since she learned how to make letters. Throughout her previous career in occupational therapy, she found herself drawn to learning the stories of her patients' lives. In 2001 she combined her interest in people's lives with her love of writing and created Write For You LLC, which has produced more than 40 memoirs for clients since its founding. She has taught memoir writing as well as children's writing workshops. Kathy lives in St. Louis, Missouri; when not working, she likes to spend time with her family, garden, and watch the birds. Find out more at www.writeforyoustl.com.

ANDY FOX

on Steven R. Covey

Though I never had the good fortune to meet Dr. Stephen R. Covey, he has been affecting my life for the better part of a quarter century. I read his best-known book, *The 7 Habits of Highly Effective People*, when it was originally published in 1989. I followed up by reading his subsequent books, including the follow-up *The 8th Habit: From Effectiveness to Greatness*, as well. Having used Franklin planners to keep meticulous track of my life for decades, I read about the merging of Dr. Covey's leadership business with Franklin Quest. Some people who have long known me describe me as detail-oriented. To my kids, who pretty much just call things as they see them, I'm "anal-retentive." Either way, I've written just about every detail down in my Franklins, and it was nice to think that Dr. Covey now had something to do with the planners I wrote it in.

But Dr. Covey became what I truly deem a mentor—someone who doesn't just teach but transforms—upon his death. That sounds paradoxical, but it's true.

Variously described as a best-selling author, prized motivational speaker, educator, entrepreneur, guru to the crème de la crème of the global business elite, and devoted family man, Dr. Covey was universally lauded for many accomplishments. By all accounts, he was a genius. He died in July 2012, several months after suffering head, rib and lung injuries from a bicycling crash that April. Dr. Covey, the tributes reported, died much too young at age 79.

It had not been many years since both my parents had passed away, so as I read about him it occurred to me that they had both been about the same age as Dr. Covey when they passed. My father wasn't a highly educated man in terms of formal schooling, but he was smart enough and determined enough to make the most of what he was given. You might say, if my dad made it wrong the first time, he used that trial to figure it out and make it to last forever the second time around. As he was being buried in 2006, I said a few words I hoped conveyed something of the heart of who he was, the essence of what made our family love him so. I may not have captured him fully, but given the unique importance of the occasion, I tried.

My mom's father, whom everybody called "Pop-Pop," had always wanted to live to be 100. He just made it past that birthday. I flew out to Tucson to meet my mom for his funeral. For reasons too complex to go into here, the prior year, one of my mom's brothers had transplanted Mom-Mom and Pop-Pop to Arizona, away from the Florida home a few blocks from my parents' where they had lived happily, and been lovingly cared for by my folks, for decades.

By the time Mom and I arrived, her brother had already arranged Pop-Pop's funeral service, and it didn't include family speakers. In the funeral home's chapel, Mom-Mom—then 99, and one of my favorite people in the world—sat in a first-row pew, directly in front of my mother. After the minister got two or three minutes into his eulogy, Mom-Mom started hissing, "No. No. No. Stop. Stop!"

Mom-Mom had a temper, but she was much too proper a person to interrupt a funeral without good reason. The story the minister was telling of Pop's-Pop's life was wrong. What had really enraged her, to the point where she forced the minister to abandon his remarks, wasn't his limited knowledge of the details of Pop's-Pop's life, however. It was Mom-Mom's realization that he wasn't accurately conveying the gist, the heart, of who Pop-Pop really was to all of us.

After the service hastily concluded, Mom-Mom sat in the parlor receiving condolences. I was last in the line of surviving family to speak with her. When I reached her, though, I couldn't think of much to say. I offered to come out to visit in several months, to help out. "Don't," she told me, "now that Pop is gone, I won't be long." My mother and I flew home the next day. Mom-Mom's words were not just heartbreaking but prophetic. I never saw her alive again.

The *New York Times* obituary of Dr. Covey included these words:

> Mr. Covey hated to waste time. He made copies of documents and kept them in briefcases under his desk in case he lost an original. And he liked to do more than one thing at a time. *Fortune* reported that he was once seen at a gym lying on the floor of the shower room being sprayed by three showerheads while he brushed his teeth and shaved.

Combined with the family reflections I've just shared, that made me stop and think of all the countless hours I had busily scribbled so much of everything into my planners over the years. By all accounts, Dr. Covey was a genius—brilliant and eminently sensible. Why on earth was he saving every minute multi-tasking with such crazy intensity? I couldn't answer for him, but I did grasp this: whether or not he was jotting down everything, like I did, in a planner, he was also finding time to write books that shared his deepest wisdom and changed millions of lives.

The *Times* obituary concluded:

> In explaining his second recommended habit— *Begin with the end in mind*—Mr. Covey urged people to consider how they would like to be remembered. "If you carefully consider what you want to be said of you in the funeral experience," he said, "you will find your definition of success."

How much more time had I spent scribbling in my Franklin Covey planners than it took Dr. Covey to author his many books? Just writing everything down, it occurred to me, meant nothing. Careful consideration of my "funeral experience," to use his expression, was not comforting. I believe in being hard-working and well-meaning and meticulous about the details—but was that enough to measure my life as truly successful? I began to think that maybe it would be a blessing if one day, some anonymous minister mangled what I was now feeling were the unremarkable details of my life.

So I figured I'd spend some time actually trying to understand what Dr. Covey wrote. There didn't seem to be any way that it could hurt me, and lots of ways that it could help.

A line I found among Dr. Covey's writings was at least mildly reassuring. "It's amazing how confused and distracted and misdirected so many people are," he had said. His books sold over 25 million copies globally; his audiobooks over 1 million. If I was clueless, at least I wasn't alone.

Thomas Edison (no intellectual slouch himself) once commanded: "There's a way to do this better—find it." In another passage, Dr. Covey clearly and coherently communicated the way.

> You have to decide what your highest priorities are and have the courage—pleasantly, smilingly, non-apologetically, to say "no" to other things. And the way you do that is by having a bigger yes burning inside. The enemy of the "best" is often the "good."

The "yes" burning up Dr. Covey's insides must have been really blazing, overwhelming multiple shower heads, 12-hour days, whatever speed how-fast-can-I-safely-bicycle-down-this-mountain-road was, and innumerable other things.

It's good news for someone just beginning to "get it" this late in life (at age 61, I'm hoping timeless is the new timely) that Dr. Covey fervently believed every one of us possesses the endowments that offer "the ultimate human freedom": the power "to choose, to respond, to change"—and also, as he said in *The 8th Habit*, the ability to "find your voice and inspire others to find theirs."

This summer marked four years after Dr. Covey's passing. I am just as unable to imagine being without my Franklin Covey planner today as I was in 2012. But I hope that what's recorded there now reflects more of my own "yes." If that hope is granted, it will be thanks in some part to Dr. Steven Covey.

The scribble in my planners looks the same these days, but what's being scribbled is totally different.

The scribbler looks the same, but he's totally different, too.

Live, love, laugh, leave a legacy. —*Dr. Stephen R. Covey*

Life's tragedy is that we get old too soon and wise too late. —*Ben Franklin*

Don't worry that children never listen to you; worry that they are always watching you. —*Robert Fulghum*

If you would not be forgotten…either write things worth reading, or do things worth writing. —*Ben Franklin*

Your most important work is always ahead of you, never behind you. —*Dr. Stephen R. Covey*

A Phi Beta Kappa graduate of the University of North Carolina at Chapel Hill, **ANDY FOX** taught public secondary school special needs students and managed manufacturing and maintenance operations in two different industries before becoming a registered financial advisor. In that role, he served as senior vice-president for a top investment firm, specializing in retirement plans and financial planning. Helping one of his twins through a 13-month treatment program for life-threatening cancer at Duke Children's Hospital has given Andy a special interest in both the work of healing institutions and the importance of expressing and preserving personal legacy. Andy is a partner in Stories of You Books, which publishes stories that connect, in anthologies that endure, with impact that transforms. The father of three grown children, Andy lives in Pinehurst, NC with his wife Susan. Find out more about Andy and his work at www.storiesofyou.org.

RAYMOND HENGERER

on William A. Kent

I got into the pool design profession by chance. A friend from my hometown of Buffalo offered me a job in the field when I was 25. It sounded like a great adventure if nothing else. I didn't really approach it as a long-term commitment—I had no idea that it would turn out to suit me and my skill set so well.

Decades later I still I enjoy the ability to work outdoors, the emphasis on teamwork and collaboration, the variety of clients and colleagues, and the always-changing aesthetic and technical challenges. The chance to meet and be inspired by a person as exceptional as Bill Kent has made me even more grateful for my choice of profession.

I've known Bill for over twenty-five years now. In the late 1980s I was working in the pool and spa business in Vero Beach, Florida, where I live, so I interacted often with Bill's wholesale pool and spa supplies distribution company. Back then, it was only a single facility in Fort Lauderdale. Today, Team Horner® is a large employee-owned family of companies and a global leader in spa and pool supplies.

Bill came to Florida from Ohio in the early 1970s. After some years designing rocket motor components he entered the swimming pool business, which he saw as a growth opportunity. I believe I first met him personally at a Florida Swimming Pool Association show. Even back then, you had the sense that he was going to be tremendously successful. Wickedly smart, hard working, interested: he just had what it takes.

The Horner employees I met loved their jobs and did them well. I would think, "Good Lord, this would be a great company to work for." The timing for that never worked out—by the time Horner had a location near enough to where I live, I had started my own firm, Agua Vida Pool Designs. But I've tried to adapt what I've learned from Bill and his organization in my own leadership and company.

Over time, my wife Linda and I have been able to take a couple of the pool cruises that Team Horner® has sponsored. I've earned CEU credits at the onboard classes, met great new people, and gotten to know the Horner team better, from the sales reps all the way to upper management. The concept of the cruises—getting everyone away from land and from their everyday obligations—is so smart. The concept perfectly demonstrates how Bill goes about things: figuring out innovative ways to get all kinds of good people involved with each other and the industry.

Seeing Bill in social situations, I've glimpsed new aspects of him. His laugh is unique and he can be lighthearted, even goofy. The first time I saw that side of him, I thought, "Oh, man. This guy's got a giant global business going here, but he doesn't take himself too seriously." That's something I really appreciate. Beyond that, he's approachable, unassuming, and likeable—always professional, but also totally down to earth.

Every time I go to the annual Florida Pool Association Show over in Orlando, I look to see if Bill's leading one of the classes. I just know there›s going to be that one or more really valuable nuggets I'm going to take away. Among other things, he's motivated me to work *on* rather than just *in* my business. Not easy, but a big difference and a big improvement.

It's possible to be a great businessperson without understanding economics or economic trends. Bill has a definite knack for both. In 2015 he added a Ph.D. in economics to his earlier B.A. (in physics) and M.B.A., an achievement that blew me away. His business savvy and feel for what's coming are extraordinary; he can astutely assess what's happening right in front of him, yet also sense much larger changes.

For example, I remember him telling me in 2005, "The downturn is going to happen, and when it does, remember this: 'Fire fast, hire slow.'" I probably didn't listen as fully or quickly as I should have. But there's no doubt that his insight helped Agua Vida survive crushingly tough times and taught me a lot about helping my business weather economic storms.

Three characteristics make Bill an especially powerful role model for me. The first is his far-reaching, innovative vision of the pool and spa industry. Bill opened my eyes to the poor image the industry had during the late eighties into the nineties. We were definitely looked down upon, and Bill has worked tirelessly to change that. He was in the forefront of getting people in my field to understand that if we wanted to improve our industry's reputation, it was up to us.

His attitude has always been, "Hey, we're not just 'pool people.' We can make people's lives better." The classes and presentations he has given or sponsored have introduced me to some of the most innovative work on water features being done around the world. I've seen the artistry, ingenuity and creativity that are possible.

Thanks in part to what he and Team Horner® have taught me, I've become more and more fascinated by working with water over the years. It's such a powerful and versatile element. Even when you're not touching it, it can soothe you with sound or delight your eyes. Bill's approach always reminds me that our job is to encourage our clients to show us enough of their souls to get their vision achieved in a way that genuinely enhances their lives.

The second characteristic is the team concept Bill's leadership embodies. I can honestly say that I›ve never talked to any Horner employee who has had anything but great things to say about their company or who is less than enthusiastic about working within it. Bill and his leadership really "walked the walk" on being a team way before most other companies thought to do so. Promoting from within whenever possible, flexible scheduling, family movie nights, on-site fitness and education classes: the list goes on.

Most importantly, I see Bill as a key mentor and role model because of the ways that he and his company have given back to the community. Team Horner® have run annual golf tournaments to raise money for the Marian Center down in Miami Gardens for 25 years or more—I've had the privilege to play in 22 of them. I›m sure that I don›t see even half of the other charitable things his companies do. What I can see is that giving back is done on a consistent basis and that participation is organization-wide. It's not just the Sales and Marketing Department putting on a show for good press. People from the warehouse, drivers, administrators—everybody joins in.

In part inspired by that model, I've been organizing an annual golf tournament to aid an area charity for 11 years now. The Arc of Indian River County provides comprehensive programs supporting special needs individuals and their families in the county in which I live and work. My connection with helping individuals with special needs goes back to my high school days. That's the first time I really interacted with them as a group, realized that they had not asked for the tough hand they were dealt, and saw the joy and courage they displayed despite their challenges. I'm proud of the tens of thousands of dollars we've raised to improve lives and the added visibility we've helped give a great cause.

More recently, I've also been able to help support the Live Like Cole Foundation here in Vero Beach. Honoring and memorializing the life of "Cole" Coppola, who died tragically young in an accident on one of our bridges, the foundation promotes kindness as a way of life in communities everywhere. It's been an honor to talk with them about what I can do to help them with new possibilities like sponsoring their own golf tournament, as well as to support initiatives such as the Cole Coppola Memorial Fishing Pier.

Contributors can choose the permanent inscriptions on "their" pier plank. The one Linda and I funded reads "in loving memory of mom and dad" over our names. To be able to leave a tangible mark on our community—something that will survive us—while helping a family heal, honoring our own families, and supporting a foundation dedicated to doing good work: in my opinion, that's the kind of legacy one should strive for.

Giving back to the community has always been important to me, though the rewards of doing so are not something you can always convey to people unless they've experienced the joy of it themselves. The older I get, the more essential it feels to leave positive change behind: to close the circle, to give back in the way that people have given to me. It's not about the money; money is just a tool. Obviously, the more tools you have, the more you can do. But if that's where the only emphasis is, for me it all misses the point. I like to think that I would be make giving back a priority even if I had never met Bill Kent, but there's no doubt that his example inspired me in that direction.

It's amazing how often I think about Bill or one of the other exceptional people from Team Horner®. I'm a better businessman and water shaper because of what I've learned from Bill Kent, and I think I'm a better person as well.

RAYMOND HENGERER was born in Lackawanna, New York. Raised by Patricia and George Hengerer with an emphasis on a good work ethic and strong moral compass, he lived in the states of New York, California, and Georgia before finding his home in Vero Beach, Florida. Ray owns and operates Agua Vida Services, a full-service pool contracting company offering pool and spa services from building to cleaning pools. Agua Vida serves its community with the mission, "Give back to the community that gives to us," a motto that also reflects Ray's enduring personal commitment to supporting charitable and community causes in the Indian River County area and beyond. His pastimes include golfing, guitar playing, and enjoying sports and social life with his wife, the writer Linda Gordon Hengerer. Find out more about Ray and his work at www.aguavidafl.com.

JAMES R. HICKS, JR.

on Abraham Bettinger

n early 1968 I was 25 years old and had been working at my first
job for nine months. My position was at a solid company in the
heart of New York City, but I had realized that it wasn't leading
me toward the future that I had envisioned. By then, I had gotten
my undergraduate degree in business from Bucknell University,
earned my M.B.A. at the University of Maryland after serving two
years in the U.S. Army, and begun pursuing my doctorate in banking
and finance at New York University's Graduate School of Business.
After years of hard work and planning, I was eager for a position
that would utilize my skills and enable me to grow.

My dad, a longtime Mobil Oil executive and my first mentor,
recommended that I find a good search firm. I did, and it sent me
on a series of interviews with organizations that seemed promising.
When I was told of an opportunity at Manufacturers Hanover Trust
Company (MHTCo), I wasn't sure it was a good fit for me. MHTCo
was the fourth largest bank in the country at that time, but I had

never pictured myself in banking. Luckily, I decided to do the interview anyway.

MHTCo was headquartered in midtown Manhattan, but the bank also had space at 59 Broad Street, within the financial district at the southern tip of Manhattan. On my way upstairs at 59 Broad, I passed what was then called the New York Commodities Exchange on the street level. The trading floor was pandemonium and seemed to be running amuck with frenetic energy, as though the wildness and din of a middle-school playground had been transplanted into the heart of Wall Street. I was glad to reach the quieter offices ten floors above.

I was interviewing with Abraham Bettinger, a Vice President at MHTCo. A pleasant, balding man in his mid-30s, he had an M.B.A. from New York University and had been with the bank since 1962. He had created a new Operations Research Group designed to use computers and a wide variety of mathematical techniques to automate and analyze various areas of the bank. It was a vision ahead of its time. Remember, this was a year before Neil Armstrong walked on the moon; seven years before Microsoft was founded; and nine full years before Apple launched its first mass-produced personal computer, a boxlike beige contraption with only a tiny fraction of the computing capacity of today's Apple Watch.

Looking at my résumé, Mr. Bettinger surprised me by commenting that I had the kind of background that would be an asset to his new group. They would mostly be mathematicians and computer specialists (the term "nerd" was just gaining widespread popularity), while I would provide the business knowledge needed to help them understand the various areas and functions of the bank. I came to understand that he didn't hire defensively or assume that everyone in a unit must have the same skills. He understood that this group would be forging new paths, and he had the confidence to hire smart people even if their prior experience was not identical to the work he wanted them to do. In fact, I would discover that his right-hand-man, Bob Beaven, was a former high school math teacher.

Mr. Bettinger showed me the mainframe computers we would use, commented that he reported directly to the Vice-Chairman of the Board, and assured me that top management was behind the Operations Research Group. When I shook his hand at the interview's end, I had a good feeling about him and the opportunity the position represented. A few days later I received a nice offer from the bank. I accepted immediately, resigned from my existing job, and two weeks later started work at MHTCo.

During my early months under his management, I discovered that having hired smart people, Abe's style was to step back and let them do their work once he had carefully articulated it. (He asked us to call him Abe, a mark of his informal style.) He was well-informed as to progress and ready to arrange any assistance that was required, but he didn't micromanage. Nor was he one for large or time-consuming meetings. Contact with his people was usually one-on-one, enabling him to probe a project's status firsthand. If there were any problems, he was always right there to get things back on track.

He was an intense, intelligent man with a quick-moving mind. It was possible to earn a stern rebuke from him—if his face got red, we knew trouble was coming—but I never remember him raising his voice to our group. (The contrast to the rowdy and aggressive Commodities Exchange, which I passed every time I went in and out of the building, couldn't have been greater.) Though measured and businesslike in manner, Abe had a vivid sense of humor and a seemingly unending supply of jokes and funny stories. He had a knack for sharing these in moments when levity would relieve tension or bolster our esprit de corps. I also remember sitting with Abe and Bob Beaven swapping our latest jokes until we roared with laughter—but then getting back to business.

Like all great mentors, Abe did everything he could to help us grow and succeed, as a group and individually. He arranged for us to have the best training possible: IBM seminars on new computer programs, for example, and industry sessions on trends in banking, taxation, pending government regulations, and the like. I remember seeing Montreal, among other places, for the first time during such events. Sometimes Abe would go to a conference with one or more members of our group, and often he was a speaker. He wanted us to be as comfortable standing up to speak about our projects as he was, a skill that was helpful to me later in my career.

Wining and dining clients, and drinking with colleagues, were definitely part of Wall Street culture at that time. Abe was not one for excess, but the occasional special gathering helped build our unit's cohesion. Our birthdays were celebrated with lunch at Fraunces Tavern, where George Washington said farewell to his officers after the Revolutionary War, or at other iconic restaurants. (Fraunces Tavern is now a museum, which seems appropriate since I now feel old enough to be a museum exhibit.) I recall the time we saw the musical *Grease* when it first started playing at The Gaiety, an old burlesque house in Greenwich Village, long before it became a Broadway hit.

During my early years at MHTCo, a financial strategy called leveraged leasing was a brand new and highly profitable area for the bank. Bob Beaven, not just an ace mathematician but also someone who expertly helped me navigate MHTCo's complexities, was developing a proprietary computer program to analyze leveraged leasing transactions. Abe agreed that Bob should show me how the program functioned, giving me an "assist" that helped propel my career over the next decade and more.

When the bank's once-tiny Leasing Department was spun off into a subsidiary called Manufacturers Hanover Leasing Corporation (MHLC) in 1972, the experience I had gained working with Abe and Bob won me a position within it. In a relatively short time I became a Vice President of MHLC, negotiating financings for aircraft, cargo and container ships, drilling rigs, and other equipment. In 1978 I negotiated the purchase of MHTCo's new headquarters at 270 Park Avenue from Union Carbide for $111 million, a very substantial sum at the time. None of this would have been possible had not Abe Bettinger seen opportunity in new fields and technologies—and potential in me.

Expert as he was on the technical side of our work, Abe never failed to respect the human side as well. As I moved from MHLC to Wall Street investment firms and had the privilege of hiring and supervising staff of my own, I always tried to follow the example Abe had given me. Hire smart people, give them the support and also the freedom they need to succeed, create an informal atmosphere, and help others grow toward their own personal goals: these and the other practices he modeled for me led to many productive working relationships, as well as friendships with former colleagues that last to this day.

I have my mentor, Abe Bettinger, to thank for that, as for so much else.

Raised in Chatham, New Jersey, **JAMES R. HICKS, JR**. earned his B.S. in business from Bucknell University. He earned his M.B.A. at the University of Maryland after being stationed as a U.S. Army officer at the Pentagon. Jim spent his career working at New York City financial services firms including Manufacturers Hanover Trust Company, E.F. Hutton and Dean Witter Reynolds, specializing in leveraged leasing and other tax-advantaged investments. The father of two grown children—who have 4 children of their own between them—Jim lives in North Carolina with his partner Carole and their two dogs.

SUE HOLBROOK

on Clyde Kennedy

Stepping through the gate, I made my way around the pool, through the sliding door and into the family room. As usual, she was sitting in the big recliner, her permanent spot when she was not in bed. Her legs were propped up and she waved the TV remote in her hand. She was delighted to see me, just as I was delighted to see her.

I can't begin to fathom what my life would have been like without my Aunt Clyde. That's right…a woman named Clyde. It's a funny name for a funny woman, and she appreciated the joke.

Having someone close to me who represented fun and laughter made all the difference in my life when I was young. Not that my parents were totally dour. They wanted fun and they did laugh, but it didn't come readily to them. Our family needed somebody to lead us to lightheartedness and joy.

And that somebody came to us when Daddy's brother, Uncle Tom, married Clyde. I've reveled in Clyde's sense of adventure as an adult. But I think it was in childhood that I needed it the most.

Being so "in the moment" themselves, kids crave the presence of people like Clyde and the sense of wonder and magic those folks bring with them.

Tom and Clyde themselves never had children, but they had a passel of nieces and nephews who loved being in their presence and in their home. How fully they allowed us—indeed, welcomed us—to pass in and out of their house (just across the street from our own) amazes me to this day. It was rare that we were sent home or that a door was locked, which gives you an idea of their love and patience.

Both were extraordinary women, but Clyde was the antithesis of my mother. Mom was intense, strong-willed, and always working. She had little time or attention for things like books, movies, sports and TV shows. Clyde, on the other hand, let herself enjoy such frivolities. She worked as hard as anyone when she worked—but when she was finished, she was ready to have fun. Even better, she shared that fun with us. I'll never forget when Tom and Clyde got a TV. It was the early 1950s, so our neighborhood still had very few sets. With Clyde, I reveled in the exciting world of *The Honeymooners*, *Topper*, and *I've Got a Secret*. Those hours were filled with laughter, camaraderie, and relaxation. There was no judgment and no pressure to do anything but sit and enjoy. It's probably because of her that today, I can manage to forgo the to-do list long enough to enjoy mundane pleasures like a good book or a deliciously bad television show.

Traveling with Tom and Clyde, too, was a treat not to be missed. Clyde's motto: "Everything's an adventure!" Clyde taught me how to travel. I mean that literally; some of my earliest travels were taken with my parents, my brother, Aunt Clyde and Uncle Tom. I got most of my sense of how to act on the road and most of my sense of the majesty of God's wide world at her side. Later, Clyde, then widowed, traveled widely. Even better, she often took my husband Ed and me along with her. It was because of Clyde that I saw Rome, experiencing the glories of St. Peter's and the Sistine Chapel among thousands of other pilgrims. I saw Las Vegas and its very different pilgrims at her side as well.

But Clyde's approach to travel also taught me deeper lessons, not just about travel but also about life. She understood the nature of both: the ups and downs, the disappointments and delights, the need for energy and adaptability and acceptance. Traveling with her, you couldn't help but grasp that no matter how wonderful a trip might be, it wouldn't reflect the glossy tourist brochures. She knew, and communicated through her every action, that perfection wasn't the point. And whatever the flaws or even calamities of the last journey, she was always planning her next trip.

The picture of Clyde that will always remain in my head is of her seated comfortably in a leather lounge chair in front of huge picture windows watching our ship pass through the Panama Canal. She was elderly by then, and not very mobile at all. Ed and I were the ones to run all over the ship, catching the details of the locks and watching for the sights on the shore. Out of necessity, Clyde stayed put. Another woman of her age and fragility level might have stayed at home. But crossing the Panama Canal was one of the things on her bucket list; she was determined to do it, and we were privileged to share it with her.

She took in every detail of the crossing, which is a long one. We started through the canal shortly after 8 a.m. and sailed into the Pacific Ocean about 3 p.m. Along the way, Ed and I took her some lunch and held her seat so she could take a restroom break without losing her front-row view. Not one whit of her attention was focused on things she couldn't do or see. To be there at all—to experience this famous place and passage she had read about—that's what Clyde wanted. Even if she experienced it from a chair. It was an adventure—and if it was both unforgettable and comfortable, that was all the better.

All of the journeys Ed and I have made have been unforgettable, but not all have been comfortable. We've arrived for a dream vacation only to discover that the airline had lost every bit of our luggage except Ed's golf bag. As we learned, you can't wear a five iron, and golf towels don't cover much. We've been drinking in the soulful silence of a Barcelona Sunday morning—and then been attacked by thieves who disappeared with the watch that had been on Ed's arm every day since his mother and I had given it to him decades before.

To the extent I managed to retain either my manners or my zest for travel in such moments, I have Aunt Clyde to thank. In such moments, the follow-up to her often-repeated mantra, "Everything's an adventure," would come into my mind. She would laugh as she added, "It might be a good adventure, it might be a bad adventure. But it's an adventure."

At home or abroad, everything's an adventure. Even the adventures we didn't actually want, with the limitations and fears and pains and surprises we didn't expect to face. Those are the times in which we grow the most. We just have to understand that the ups and downs are in the nature of things—the rule, and not the exception.

Since I first started to write down my memories of her, Clyde has passed on. The house with the pool has been sold and her possessions, including that recliner, shared out among family and friends and a deserving charity. But she lives on in my memory and, I hope, my spirit. When I can laugh at myself, embrace the unexpected, stop to drink in the wonder of God's creation, or take a snafu in stride, I like to think that I'm paying homage to her zesty, joyful essence. And meanwhile, I have no doubt that Clyde herself is savoring the most extraordinary adventure of all.

SUE HOLBROOK is a wife, mother, grandmother, and lay speaker in the Florida Conference of the United Methodist Church. A native Floridian who describes her writing, speaking and teaching work as sharing "God's Glory...with a side of grits," Sue encourages women to find the inspiration and strength in their own God histories. Sue is the author of *Faith Breezes: Glimpsing God's Glory in Everyday Life*; she is currently working on a follow-up book, *Scattered Storms*, as well as a collection of stories drawn from Biblical figures. Find out more about Sue's book and speaking, and read her blog, at www.sueholbrook.net.

CYNTHIA HURST

on Lydia Woodruff

first encountered Professor Lydia Woodruff—born in Rimini, Italy as Francesca Ambrosina Lydia Solaroli—in 1973 as a student in her Humanities course at Michigan State University. After a couple of meetings during her office hours we clicked, and she began to take me under her wing.

In my eyes, she was truly *Italian*. I italicize the word to emphasize that it was more than just a nationality. Being *Italian* meant that she possessed both the ability to see to the heart of things and an engaging continental charm. She had deep brown eyes that contained a hint of laughter but saw everything, a Roman nose, a warm smile of greeting. She wore good-quality dresses or blouses with midi-length skirts, sensible shoes or low-heeled pumps—never pants. Her long, dark hair was pinned up in a French twist until she turned fifty, when she had it cut in a chin-length bob. That took years off her, and I think she felt quite pleased with herself.

Being *Italian* also meant being a natural cynic—though a soulful one. Regarding the Catholic Church her comment was, "We sell it, but we don't believe it!" By the 1970s Italy had excellent national health care, paid parental leave, and other advances Americans were still not in agreement on, much less providing. But the Americans were the cowboys, the mavericks, the innovators. We had enthusiasm, generosity, and true grit admired throughout the world. "I don't care what anybody says," Lydia would proclaim. "Everyone wants to be American!"

Mrs. Woodruff would often walk into the classroom, go to the blackboard, pick up a piece of chalk, and start our class by writing something like one of the following:

There is no God.

Man can do anything.

Everything we do is Roman. Everything we think is Greek.

Character is destiny.

Mediocrity is worse than failure.

These provocative statements were meant to make us question, to hone our beliefs, to build character, and to awaken us to the limitless world outside ourselves. (I should add that she used Mozart and Salieri as an example for the *mediocrity is worse than failure* discussion long before *Amadeus* was ever a popular play or film.)

Research, research, research—painstakingly done, before the days of computers or the Internet, smart phones or iPads: that was the secret of her lectures. Voltaire's mother lived in the room next to his. His mistress lived in the room on the other side of his. She acted as though this was very funny, but everything she told us challenged us in some way to think about the absurd situations life presents to us and how we would respond.

She often mentioned Jean Paul Sartre and Simone de Beauvoir for their humanistic and thought-provoking approach to life. Nietzsche's "what doesn't kill us makes us stronger" was a favorite quote. Professor Woodruff loved the existentialists because they advanced philosophical thought through work based in passion mixed with struggle. That, for her, was the perfect combination.

Lydia was not without spirituality, however. Her cynicism came from the hypocrisy, greed, bureaucracy, and power—in the name of religion and politics—she had viewed throughout history and experienced herself. She felt called to lead what Socrates called the examined life. She believed the greatest of the philosophers and scientists, artists, and saints were inventors, thinkers, and experimenters who looked beyond the standards of the times to reach for more. She considered the 1969 Apollo 11 moon launch—the liftoff of which she witnessed at Cape Canaveral along with her physicist husband, Truman, and other distinguished scientists and spectators—a true mystical experience.

When I met her she drove a gray Fiat. The letters of that brand, according to her, stood for "Fix It Again, Tony!" With a red leather interior, a sporty engine, and a stick shift, it was her little tribute to Italy. Occasionally we would go to the farmer's market together in that car. With Lydia, everything was an adventure. First stop was always a crisp apple to eat while we perused the stalls. Lydia knew all the vendors and talked and joked with several of them as she filled her tote bag with berries, vegetables, herbs and flowers. As a student living on soup, omelets and bar food, I found this to be a delightfully sensual whole-foods shopping experience.

There was a high-end department store called Jacobson's across M.A.C. Avenue facing the campus. The store featured New York-caliber window displays, designer fashions, quality merchandise, personalized service, and, on the top floor, a wonderful restaurant surrounded by windows with a view of the tree-lined street. All of the salespeople knew Lydia, so when we went there together we would breeze through the store like VIPs, chatting up the staff and looking at extravagant things. On one trip we found a small, rose-embellished pink alabaster box made in Italy that I was enthralled with. Being very modern in attitude and style, Lydia could not understand my attraction to this antique-looking item, but she purchased it for me and I have it to this day, a fond remembrance of her.

At Christmastime Lydia would either stop by the bookstore where I worked (close friends with the owners, she had arranged for my interview there) or ask me to drop by her house on my way home. She would then present me with a box of chocolates—always white chocolate bonbons with dark chocolate mousse centers, which I adored—a bouquet of holly, or some other holiday treat.

One Sunday I took my parents to meet her and Truman. The Woodruff home was in East Lansing, built into a small hill on one street corner. The decor was stylishly modern, with white shag carpeting, white walls, black and chrome furniture, a yellow master bedroom, a fully-equipped kitchen, and colorful and whimsical art everywhere. There was a terraced garden and pool in the back, and that's where we met for tea and conversation. My mother marveled at the beauty of the house and garden. It was a lifestyle she could not imagine. She told her hostess, "You have so many beautiful things!" Lydia replied, "But you see, your children are your jewels!"

A mentorship offers the opportunity for both the mentor and the protégé to grow through the relationship in profound and unexpected ways. Lydia gave me an international perspective, an introduction to the joys of food and entertaining, and a sense of the richness of science and the humanities. She also taught me, by example, about survival. Only an indomitable spirit such as hers could survive the tragedies—from war and near starvation to culture shock, miscarriages and car accidents—she had experienced. Lydia's great zest for life and learning surmounted all obstacles.

In turn, I gave her an American friend who reminded her of herself, humorous anecdotes to share, and the daughter she never had. I think she liked that I was from a large Catholic family and a quick study striving to achieve with her guidance. I loved her sense of humor, her Italian accent, the thirst for knowledge she shared with the world, and her exuberance for life. Together we were, as she loved to say, *a pretty good deal.*

CYNTHIA HURST grew up in a large family in Detroit. She has worked as a bookstore manager, a lobbyist assistant for Lear-Siegler, and a procurement and contracts manager with the State of Michigan. After raising two sons in the East Lansing area, Cynthia married successful inventor Richard Hurst. They moved to Vero Beach, Florida, where they enjoyed a life dreams are made of and shared the adventures of writing and world travel prior to his death in 2015. Cynthia is the author of four books. The first two are travel memoirs. The second two, *The Diamond Project* and *The Platinum Project*, feature the sparkle and strength of women and men today. Next, she is contemplating an exploration of our search for spirituality called *The Star Project*.

BILL KEETON

on Burnell Brown

When I was at the University of Mississippi Medical School in the 1960s, I spent a good portion of my last two years trying to decide what area of medicine to go into. I fluctuated between OB/GYN, surgery, psychiatry, and neurology; I even considered pediatrics for about 20 minutes before I came to my senses. I never gave anesthesiology much thought, taking for granted that it would be pretty boring just sitting there while the patient was asleep.

But once I was actually exposed to the field, I knew that this was my calling. I was interested enough in pharmacology to have done a year's research in it, and anesthesiology and pharmacology are closely linked. I quickly realized that anything that could happen to patients while they are awake can also happen to them while under anesthesia—the difference is that anesthetized patients can't explain their symptoms. An anesthesiologist must diagnose the problem instantly, and correctly, if the patient is to survive.

Once I finished my internship I headed to Dallas to do my anesthesiology residency at Parkland Memorial Hospital. Famous as the hospital that tried to save President Kennedy, Parkland was one of the best-known trauma centers in the US. At the time I was there, Dallas had a very active "knife and gun club" that supplied us with a plethora of patients and kept several operating rooms constantly busy almost every night. The workload was grueling, but the experience it gave a resident was incredible.

Shortly after I started my anesthesia training I learned that I would be assigned to the pain clinic some Thursday afternoons. I wasn't happy. Despite having watched my father suffer courageously for over a decade with chronic intractable neck pain, I admit that I assumed all the pain-clinic patients were whiners, hypochondriacs or people just trying to get out of work.

Dr. Burnell Brown and a sweet 78-year-old lady named Mrs. Newman changed that deplorable attitude permanently. First, Dr. Brown. After graduating from the Tulane University School of Medicine, Burnell Brown had completed his anesthesiology residency at Parkland. He then joined the academic staff at Parkland and simultaneously entered the Ph.D. program in pharmacology. Our mutual interests in anesthesiology and pharmacology gave us a lot in common. So did the fact that we were both students—me in medicine, he in pharmacology—at the same time, even though he was also my instructor and mentor. If you think that sounds confusing, you're probably right.

Dr. Brown was married with children, so I can't imagine how he even found time to button his shirt in the morning, much less earn a Ph.D. while teaching medicine. Yet I can't remember his ever seeming rushed or in a hurry. He was consistently relaxed, always able to find time to help others, and calm when doing tricky procedures like celiac plexus blocks, which are difficult even with today's advanced imaging devices.

He was also unusual in staying in the hospital until 11 p.m. on the nights when he was on staff call. That wasn't required, and except for Burnell and another exceptional professor named Ted Bennett, the staff rarely did it. Being actually present rather than just on call when the residents were seeing patients at night, Drs. Brown and Bennett gave us invaluable hands-on guidance.

Dr. Brown was in charge of the Parkland pain clinic, which brings me back to Mrs. Newman. She was very frail due to terminal cancer, which had metastasized to her lower spine. She would limp into the clinic hunched over at the waist, moaning with each step. There was absolutely no doubt in my mind that her pain was real and excruciating.

One day in 1967, Dr. Brown instructed me to place Mrs. Newman face down on the examining table with a pillow under her hips. He then pointed to an area over her tailbone and instructed me to press it with my index finger. Doing as instructed, I was horrified when Mrs. Newman responded with a scream of agony. Before I could even apologize, Dr. Brown instructed me to inject this area with a solution of cortisone and local anesthetic. Again, I did as instructed. Again, she let out a horrific scream. I felt terrible. I didn't want to be in the pain clinic in the first place and I certainly didn't want to add to this poor woman's misery.

By now I was furious with Dr. Brown. I pictured myself storming out of the clinic and heading straight for the department chairman's office to report this behavior and save Dallas from further sadistic torture.

Sensing my dissatisfaction, Dr. Brown looked at me and with a knowing grin and a wink of the eye. "Bill," he said, "why don't you help Mrs. Newman sit up?" Surprisingly, she seemed to sit up and get off the table with relative ease. Tentatively at first, she turned from side to side. Next she began to walk around the room, now standing straight rather than hunching over.

And then, a huge smile on her face, she took my hand and swung me into a dance—it might have been the Virginia Reel, though I can't say for sure—laughing and singing a bit of a tune as I tried to keep up with her.

I can honestly say that my life changed at that moment. I have been treating pain and designing educational programs around pain management ever since.

After that day, I don't think I ever missed a single opportunity to go to the pain clinic. I followed the "wicked" Dr. Brown around like a lost puppy, trying to absorb everything I could learn from him. He turned out to be not only one of the smartest gentlemen I've ever known, but also one of the nicest. In addition to all he taught me about pain treatment and anesthesiology, I should add that he was my ethnic food mentor as well. Growing up in 1940s Jackson, Mississippi, I hadn't had much exposure to Chinese or Mexican food. Both my ability to use chopsticks and my weekly cravings for burritos are due to his expert "instruction."

I continued to follow Mrs. Newman, treating her with the same type of injection, until she died a few months later. Burnell became a dear friend as well as mentor. While we were both still in Dallas, I enjoyed visits to Helen and Burnell Brown's home. (He loved to cook Peking Duck, the recipe for which, he insisted, involved hanging the duck from a light fixture.) Later, he invited me to join his department when he became the chairman of anesthesiology at the University of Arizona in Tucson. It wasn't the right move for me at the time, but I still appreciate the profound compliment of being asked.

When my daughter Beth applied to a graduate program at that same university in 1994, my wife Dee and I visited Burnell and Helen in Tucson. The news he shared was devastating. He had returned from a skiing trip with what he thought was a minor back problem, but diagnostic imaging showed that he had metastatic cancer. At the time of our visit he estimated that he had about eight months to live. He said all of this calmly, in the same matter of fact tone and relaxed manner I remembered. There was no drama or self-pity, just thoughtful planning about how best to use his remaining time. Though we spoke on the phone thereafter, that was the last time I saw him before he died the following year.

I can't thank Dr. Brown or Mrs. Newman enough. They set me on a path that has given me a fascinating career and, more importantly, allowed me to help many patients suffering with intractable pain. For that, and for the chance to know someone as remarkable as Burnell Brown, I feel truly fortunate. As I write this, it has been almost fifty years since that pivotal afternoon in 1967. But I have thought of both of Dr. Brown and Mrs. Newman virtually every day since, and always with profound gratitude and appreciation.

DR. BILL KEETON received his M.D. degree from the University of Mississippi Medical School. He served in the US Air Force as Chief of Anesthesia and Chief of the Pain Clinic, which he established at Westover AFB, Massachusetts. After serving as Chief of Anesthesia at DeKalb Medical Center in Atlanta for 15 years, Dr. Keeton became the founder and director of DeKalb Pain Center from 1984 until he joined Pain Consultants of Atlanta in August of 2007. A frequent lecturer on emerging and state-of-the-art pain management, Dr. Keeton is also the author of *A Boy Called Combustion: Growing Up in 1940s Mississippi*, which won an Independent Publisher (IPPY) award for best Southern-region nonfiction. Find out more at www.billkeeton.com.

FRANCES KING

on Elizabeth Chickering King

When I was 11, I found a picture of a beautiful racehorse in a magazine. It was a contest promotion: you name the horse and you could win the horse. It was my big chance. Like most little girls, I had fallen for horses. I already knew that I'd have a leg up in the contest—maybe even a winning leg—if I enlisted my mother in the project.

Never mind that we were living in a rented house on a busy street in a college town, awaiting the completion of our own handicap-ready house, then under construction—a house that would never have more than a small rock garden for a back yard. She jumped in with her usual enthusiasm, and we spent hours trying out different names, with hers the more elegant and sophisticated—like "Narragansett," and "Roan's Pride," to my drab and dreary "Running Beauty" and other uninspiring attempts. She never expressed any doubt that we'd win, and so our entry (with the chosen name I no longer remember) went off to the post office, signed and sealed.

We didn't win.

But in hindsight, it was a small and sparkling moment for me, the value of which I didn't—couldn't—understand then or for many years afterward, perhaps even beyond her sudden early death at 63. It was one in a string of pearls she gave me throughout my childhood and young motherhood—that solid, smooth sense that I had value, and that I was worth listening to. As clichéd as it sounds, hers was the very definition of love without limits or conditions, the kind with staying power. And now I have the years to look back for proof. Was it her enforced confinement? Or had she simply come into the world with the gifts others sought out in her? I'll never know. And I don't spend time wondering; instead, I look back, cherish, and now understand how rare those gifts were.

Elizabeth Chickering was a spirited, beautiful, educated young woman when she met my father at a house party in New Hampshire, a party arranged by the Detroit-based uncle and aunt with whom she lived while attending boarding school. She'd grown up around the world, an Army brat, but high school meant staying in one spot. At 18, she fell instantly in love with John King, and finished Mount Holyoke in three years so she could become Mrs. John S. King in 1942. As he rose up the professional ladder (working at General Electric as a research physicist), she happily tended house, wrote children's books, and gave birth to three babies. Then in 1954, in the midst of the polio shockwave in America, her life changed course. At 32, she was suddenly a paraplegic, confined to wheelchair and home, reliant on others, and left to rearrange her enormous spirit from freedom to confinement. While my father was unusually supportive, attentive and loving, her work of adjusting to a radically different life entailed a solitary and deeply lonely journey.

Her journal entries from the mid-1950s, in the aftermath of polio, show a powerful determination to "beat" the disease and triumph over it. Beat it she did not. But triumph? Oh, she did, if we measure that by the welcoming face she turned to the world, the scores of people who sought her out and cherished the attention she paid them, the friends of mine who came to the house mostly to see her, not me, and the adoration in life and devastation in death she inspired in our extended family.

But I don't think she ever truly triumphed over the loneliness, poured out in the unseen and unpublished poems she wrote and squirreled away for so many years (some of them found accidently in my father's papers after his death). Only now, in middle age and with a family of my own, do I begin to understand what she did and what she lost. And what she taught. You never just "have polio"; the body continues to complain and punish and demand for many years after, eventually gifting you anew with more muscle loss, more dependence. But for me, as a child, family life still seemed pretty standard. Wasn't my mom pretty much like other moms, even though she didn't do Girl Scouts, or take me horseback riding, or go shopping with me for prom dresses? We said our prayers together at night, she took care of us when we were sick—and the standard bump-bang, bump-bang of her leg braces and Lofstrand crutches as she labored through the house were part of our growing up. (She abandoned her braces after just a few years, and greeted the world from the chair.) Still, didn't everybody else have just one parent in the audience for the play? Didn't everybody's mom have to be lifted in and out of the tub? And didn't everybody get steady love, even through the teenage deceits, thoughtless remarks, adolescent self-focus, tear-strewn disappointments and failures, stupid notes, wrong-headed and hurtful friendships, and hormonal rages?

But those poems. And those long, solo days she spent at the desk, facing the bright front lawn, people passing by, children racing, dogs barking…

She was a writer. Of poetry, essays, notes, kids' books, and hundreds upon hundreds of letters, all carefully typed (no mistakes) on the Smith Corona manual, and all bearing a tiny smiling cartoon face on the envelope. She wrote me twice a week from the day I left for college through my new marriage and motherhood, until just a few months before she died. I still have those letters, nearly every one. They are her legacy, in often humorous, deeply descriptive, sweetly colloquial, and always non-proscriptive lessons in living.

I became a writer too, but of a different sort. So was she my mentor? If by mentor, we mean someone who teaches us how to do specific things, cultivate particular skills, and define our ambitions, then no. But if we mean a kind of life-guide, a practitioner of patience and perseverance, a solitary warrior against solitude, and a devoted, prolific, and intentional communicator, then yes, she was my mentor.

Today, I know that she didn't teach me how to write. She taught me how to live.

FRANCES KING is a writer and editor with more than 30 years in journalism, publications planning and management, nonfiction writing, and editing. She fell into personal biography eight years ago, and began to help individuals and families preserve their memories in printed legacy books through her company, HistoryKeep. Building on a love of biography and story, and with many years as an interviewer, she has written or edited more than two dozen books and often teams with other personal historians as a developmental and copy editor. Francie has a B.A. in English literature from Denison University and an M.A. in social anthropology from Boston University. Find out more about Francie and her work at www.historykeep.com.

LINDA LEARY

on Paula Underwood

We sat in a circle around the room on pillows, blankets, and a chair or two for those of us whose knees and backs argued when sitting on the floor. The object of my attention, Paula Underwood, sat reading to us from one of her three "learning stories," igniting our brains and hearts with curiosity, Native American style. Her dark eyes and gray-streaked hair spoke of her Native American roots and her stories were part of the thousand-year-plus oral tradition of her father's people.

I felt like a young child in her presence, eager and wanting to hear more, full of questions for which there were no clear answers, only more questions. Her excitement was contagious and she often giggled out of sheer joy when one of us had some "aha" moment. She would end each story with the same question: "And what may we learn from this?" We would respond with many answers, depending on our perspective and life experience. "Who is right?" we would ask, hoping for a definitive winner. "All," she would reply with a playful gleam. "And what may we learn from *that?*"

Over the years she would teach us without directly teaching, sending us out into a New Mexico arroyo on mini-vision quests of observation and silence. She made a large circle on the ground, calling it the Great Hoop of Life, with the four directions of north, east, south and west all marked. We walked it clockwise, stopping at this place or that, noting where we were and what that point might signify to us based on her teaching and the question we were pondering. It always worked. And it changed, as round and round we went, pondering, questioning some issue. Paula clapped her hands in positive glee when one of us shouted, "I got it!"

Learning like this was fun. I had forgotten how to play as children play, how to just be in the moment. Who cared what others thought? We had a universe to explore under the moon and the stars and the desert grasses. On one of my mini-quests I found myself seated by a tiny pile of bleached white bones, of a vole perhaps, with a perfectly preserved little leg bone, a femur maybe. It was as if the creature had died quietly—you could still see its tiny skeleton lying in repose, waiting for this curious woman to find it and be in wonder.

One night we sat around a fire at a retreat on a northern California hilltop, our faces turned upward to the trillion stars, breathless at the sight of a rare meteor shower. Paula broke our silence by telling us that she was now going to share something precious and dear to her. We waited expectantly for some new revelation that would leave us once again pondering the deepest meaning of life. Then she said her secret dream was to sing opera to a live audience. Huh? She stood up and burst into the song "On a Clear Day, I Can See Forever" to her audience of open-mouthed students, accompanied by a few coyotes, the stars serving as her spotlights. Her voice was soprano, a bit shaky in spots, yet on key and straight from her soul. I had goose bumps, and it was a very warm night.

"I have always wanted to do that," she said, grinning like the Cheshire Cat. She curtsied and sat down. We applauded and whistled and hooted and laughed and cried, tears of joy and sharing and caring. No wonder some called her "Turtle Woman Singing." We learned of the meaning of the spirits of some animals according to her tradition and our personality traits. I was Wolf personality, the organizer, the orator. I threw caution to the wind and howled at the moon. How liberating.

Paula was eventually diagnosed with Parkinson's, which made her right hand shake uncontrollably. She would reach over and gently hold it with her left hand as if to say, "It's all right, I will hold you, don't be afraid." Walking on rough terrain was becoming more difficult and one of us always appeared by her side to assist as unobtrusively as possible, little companion ghosts moving beside her. I remember helping her sit and then sliding down to the floor by her side, reaching up to place my hand softly on the hand with the tremor, calming it for the moment. Now she had her left hand with which to gesture, most important for those of us who "talk" with our hands. It was "our" moment and she looked down and smiled, a thousand words in a glance.

Not much later her condition deteriorated. Much of her work had been done, though according to her it was just beginning. She advised us to add to the work as appropriate to circumstance, then take it out to the four directions. And we have. We live across the globe, north, east, south and west. Some of us still keep in contact on occasion after all these decades, sharing how we use our "learnings" in education, business, counseling, and family and how we transform them into something new while preserving the essence of the old—as it should be. Paula would call that adding New Eyes Wisdom to Old Eyes Wisdom. I have read one of her first learning stories, "Who Speaks for Wolf," to little children, teens and adults, always asking at the end, "And what may we learn from this?" Storytelling is a gentle and fun way to teach without forcing another's learning. Everybody has an answer. It is all right and it is all good.

Paula has moved on to be with her ancestors, yet as I write this I can hear "On a Clear Day" in my head. I still know all the lyrics, those words about clarity, rising, looking around, seeing who you are. Now if only I could carry a tune.

LINDA LEARY is a mother, grandmother, self-acclaimed "Boomer Babe" (that is, a female Baby Boomer with pizzazz), trained practitioner in restorative justice for youth and adults, and moonlight writer. For more information on Paula Underwood, visit www.learningpeople.org.

GENE LEE

on Ernest Hemingway

I n the fall of 2010 during a conversation with a friend about writers and writing, I made the comment that male writers of my generation lived and worked in the shadow of Ernest Hemingway. By "my generation" I meant those of us, born in mid-20th century, who came of age in the early 1970s—some years after the author's death, yet at a time when the man's legacy and body of work were still being hotly contested in literary quarters all over the world. My female friend, not being a Hemingway reader, didn't quite know how to respond to my comment. Being unsure myself— the remark being one of those blasts of sudden insight I hadn't seen coming—I didn't take it any further. I just knew that "Papa" had set the literary bar very high.

That fall I was just finishing up what I called the "sea section" of my novel, *Men Without Hate*. Any time in the past when I was writing about the sea, boats, men, and the elements, it seemed that Hemingway was never far from my thoughts. The first non-children's novel I ever read was his *To Have and Have Not*, which Hemingway wrote in the late 1930s. I was ten years old at the time and had found the book on my grandfather's bookshelf. When I showed him what I was going to read he just smiled and said, "Let me know what you think about it."

I enjoyed the action sections, the stoicism of one-armed Harry Morgan, and the scenes set in Key West bars and on the sea. The sparse prose made it easy for a boy of ten to read. As for the parts about men and women, I was of course lost. The action and colorful characters, though, made up for any of the stuff I didn't understand. Not long after I finished the book Hemingway killed himself and my grandfather drifted into the illness that finally took his life. I never did get the chance to tell "Pop" what I thought about it.

Through family history told me by my mother, grandfather, great aunts and great uncles, I learned that my grandfather and Hemingway were contemporaries with some things in common. Hemingway lived in Key West during the 1930s, while my grandfather lived in Ft. Lauderdale. They both loved the sea, fishing, and hunting, and both of them were caught up in the 1935 Labor Day hurricane that devastated the Keys. They shared a mutual friend—Marjorie Kinnan Rawlings, who owned and eloquently wrote about the Florida homestead Cross Creek—and late in life they both did what they could to help the Cuban exiles against Castro. Though there was no evidence to suggest that the men ever met, there was also none to suggest that they *never* did.

With their deaths so close together, for a long time—hell, even to this day—whenever I read or think of Hemingway, I think of my grandfather as well.

I didn't come across any other works by Hemingway until four years after reading that first novel. During a European trip in the summer of 1965, my family went to bullfights in both Madrid and Cordova. My mother and I loved the spectacle of the ring, the colorful matadors practicing their ancient art, the roars of the crowd, the cheers of approval when the matadors made a good kill and the jeers when they did not. When we returned home Mom bought me a copy of Hemingway's *Death in the Afternoon* and a photo-biography of El Cordobés, the famous—not to mention young and handsome—matador we had been fortunate enough to see fight in his hometown of Cordova. (It took me a while to realize that the El Cordobés book was for her and not me.) Awed by everything about Spain, I followed up *Death in the Afternoon* with *For Whom the Bell Tolls*.

At that age, I assumed that when I grew up I would follow the rest of the family into the practice of law. Something about Hemingway's works began to eat at me, though. From a young age I had been known for coming up with elaborate stories that I told the rest of the family around the dinner table. When I learned how to write, I began putting those tales down on paper. My elementary school teachers seemed impressed when I showed them what I had written, and I enjoyed the writing process. Now, after reading Hemingway's prose—the tight sentences, the vivid action and settings, the characters who were not just characters but honest-to-God living people he was able to create—got me wondering if maybe, just maybe, I too could do the same.

Another factor that appealed to me as a 14-year-old boy, of course, was the lifestyle of the famous author. A choice suddenly opened up for me: I could go on and become a lawyer, stuck in a stale career, wearing a suit, going to court and just making money. Or—and this was a big "or" for a boy my age—I could have a life of adventure, travel, hunting, fishing, and war. Not to mention the women, the drinking, and doing as I pleased. Blissfully unaware of the fact that writing for a living is incredibly hard work, the choice seemed pretty easy. Writer I became.

Over the years, in school and elsewhere, I came across other writers who struck the same chords in me that Hemingway had. Joyce, Faulkner, Wolfe—in my rebellious youth, Kerouac and the other Beats—they all played their part in my creative processes. The list of literary inspirations seems endless, actually.

But it was Hemingway who propelled me into the life I chose. I learned the hard way not to imitate him—there was only one Hemingway. Besides, who wants to be derivative? He certainly did not, and railed against his imitators all his life.

Still, I took his advice to heart: to find my own voice, and with it, to put down on paper the world as I would like it to be. In the back of my mind during all of the years I've spent trying to do just that: the vision of my grandfather and of Ernest Hemingway. Two men beside whose giant shadows the one I myself cast sometimes seems small—but also men whose examples have given me the courage to live my life all the way through. And, in Hemingway's case at least, that high bar he set for writers, which seemed to me too high when I first began to write? I came to learn that with my writing, it is I who set the bar.

Born and raised in Florida, **GENE LEE** currently lives in Indian River County. His plans to become a lawyer were derailed when at the age of 13, inspired by Ernest Hemingway and James Joyce, he began writing stories. After many years of writing and publishing his poetry in literary journals, Gene returned to his first love, fiction. His novel *Men Without Hate* follows two men from the Raines family through two very different wars and home again. When not writing he enjoys fly fishing in the Indian River for the snook, redfish, and tarpon roaming those waters and maintains a voracious and longstanding reading habit. Find out more about Gene and *Men Without Hate* at www.geneleeauthor.com.

KEN LEVINE

on Bruce Anson

Great expression in Hollywood: *Mentors get eaten by their young.*

While there is certainly no shortage of that *All About Eve*-type behavior, I must say that for myself, I would never be where I am today were it not for some exceptional mentors. It's like I learned pitching from a staff of Sandy Koufaxes: Larry Gelbart, Jim Brooks, Allan Burns, the Charles Brothers, Gene Reynolds, Tom Patchett, Jay Tarses, Treva Silverman, and one name few folks in Hollywood have ever heard—Bruce Anson. Don't race to the Internet Movie Database to look him up. He's not there. Even Googling him will yield no results. (There are others with that name but they're not him.)

But Bruce Anson taught me more about the craft of writing than all my high school and college teachers combined.

I was a sports intern at KMPC radio in Los Angeles. Bruce was one of their newscasters. He was in his 60s and smoked and drank too much (which I think was a prerequisite for getting hired in that department back then). He had been a booth announcer in the early days of TV and, prior to that, on network radio. And now he was pulling part-time Sunday night shifts, writing and delivering news twice an hour, in between public service programs the station was obligated to run. When he finished at midnight the station went off the air for maintenance. So not exactly prime time.

He'd show up in shorts, loud Hawaiian shirts, and flip-flops. Other newsmen reported for work in suits and ties.

My job was to write the sports portion of the newscast. Essentially a rundown of the day's scores. *Northwestern beat Ohio State 23-10, Notre Dame edged Army 21-20*, etc. The most creative thing I did was once write: *LSU puffed Rice 34-14.*

During baseball season all the scores would be final by 6:00 p.m. There was no Sunday night baseball. Not even in Texas. The shift went until midnight but most sports interns would write up three sportscasts that could be rotated and went home six hours early. I went to Bruce and asked if I could help write his newscasts. He said, "Sure, but it's not as easy as you think."

He was right.

I'd take a story from the United Press International wire, rewrite it, and hand it to Bruce. I assumed he'd say, "Great job. Thank you."

No.

He said, "This sentence could be cut in half," "There's a better way of saying this," "Use more descriptive words," "This point should go ahead of that point," or "This phrase is a little confusing." He'd then take a pen and start rewriting—slashing words, replacing phrases, making it shorter, punchier, clearer, BETTER.

And so began a weekly pattern that lasted until football season. I would doggedly write story after story determined to just once please that son-of-a-bitch. Finally it happened. A house fire story. I don't remember the details but I do remember I used the word "blaze." It aired right before the vasectomy PSA. I was so proud.

Be ruthless. Always look to make it better. Have a little Bruce Anson sitting on your shoulder when you write. Ask him to put out the cigarette, though.

I owe Bruce Anson a lot. I thank him for his time, his toughness, his talent. And if he were here today I'm sure he'd say, "Isn't all the alliteration a little precious?"

KEN LEVINE is an Emmy-winning writer, director, producer and Major League Baseball announcer. He is the author of plays including 2016's *Going, Going, Gone!* and books including the satirical novel *Must Kill TV; The Me Generation...By Me: Growing Up in the '60s; It's Gone...No, Wait a Minute!; and Where The Hell Am I?: Trips I Have Survived.* Ken has worked on *MASH, Cheers, Frasier, The Simpsons, Wings, Everybody Loves Raymond, Becker,* and *Dharma & Greg,* and has co-created his own series including *Almost Perfect.* He and his partner David Isaacs wrote the feature *Volunteers,* starring Tom Hanks. Ken has also been the radio/TV play-by-play voice of the Baltimore Orioles, Seattle Mariners, and San Diego Padres. The co-writer of the produced musical *The 60s Project,* Ken blogs at www.kenlevine.blogspot.com, which *TIME Magazine* named one of the Top 25 blogs of 2011.

DEBRA M. LEWIS

on James O. Scott

Lieutenant, Colonel Graves wants to see you," a staff officer told me as I reported to the 20th Engineer Brigade headquarters at Fort Bragg. The 20th was the primary engineer unit at Fort Bragg, tasked with providing support to other Army units in the form of construction, engineering, mechanical work and map-making. The Brigade Commander was five levels higher on the military chain of command than I was. "Uh oh," I thought as I obeyed the summons.

Once I was sitting in front of Colonel Graves, the reason for our meeting was revealed with typical military directness. He had decided that I would lead a platoon. Second lieutenants like I was then are lucky to get a platoon command assignment. But the platoon in question was one that had never had an officer in charge. The last non-commissioned officer (NCO) to lead it had left the platoon under a cloud, a planned reorganization was about to triple its size, and a high-visibility evaluation by the United States Army Forces Command, or FORSCOM, would be taking place within the month.

Why me? I didn't ask that question aloud, of course. But I can surmise that the fact that I had just graduated from the US Military Academy at West Point was the answer. I had been one of the 119 female cadets West Point had admitted as its first female class in 1976, and my time there had definitely not been easy. At 22, I was tough enough to lead a platoon—but this one sounded like a real challenge.

My early weeks as platoon leader were both frustrating and invigorating. I had done a thorough assessment and started rolling out my plan when I was informed that Sergeant First Class James O. Scott would be my new NCO. I learned of his arrival on the unit when several soldiers came up to report it, adding, "He's changing what you want to do and telling us to do it his way."

The last thing I needed was someone trying to countermand my orders before even so much as meeting me. When I first glimpsed him, I said crisply, "Sergeant Scott, we need to talk! Let's meet after formation." At the meeting, I promptly informed him of what I had heard. "I realize I'm young," I remember saying, "but I'm the platoon leader, and if you can't work with that, I'll find you another job."

If Sergeant Scott felt anger or defensiveness, he didn't show it. Calmly, he explained what had happened and what he was trying to do. I realized I had been wrong, doing something I never did: I had gone negative, and on absolutely no true evidence. SFC Scott's measured response turned that negativity around.

That was my introduction to some of the qualities I came to find most exceptional in SFC Scott. He had the deepest commitment to service; without ego, he simply did what was right, however difficult. Equally important, he was tremendously perceptive. He saw something good in me that ran deeper than my actions in that moment. Notwithstanding the rocky start, it wasn't long before our working relationship fell into place. We didn't need to do a lot of talking about our dealings with each other or the direction we were taking the platoon. We just clicked.

We were definitely an "odd couple." I'm a 5'5" white woman, then sporting a Dorothy Hamill-style haircut that did nothing to hide my youth. Sergeant Scott was a tall, dark-skinned black non-commissioned officer, about 39 at that time. But the superficial differences just didn't matter.

Sergeant Scott was affectionately known as Scotty or Teacup, the latter a nickname given to him by his family and friends. A North Carolina native with a lovely wife and two daughters, he had a deep voice and the best deep-hearted laugh ever. He loved people and loved what he did, which made it fun to work around him. He could be focused on solving a complicated problem one minute and playful the next. I remember the salesman for Krispy Kreme donuts coming around and Scotty chasing him away with mock toughness, knowing that I would probably buy a big box and he'd be tempted to indulge. To be in SFC Scott's presence was to be in the presence of joy.

Although Scotty lived an hour away from the base, he was at work from early morning to late at night. If you needed some specialized expertise, Scotty either had it or knew where to find it—he seemed to know everyone on the installation and loved making connections between people. Yet he could be tough when necessary. You sensed you couldn't get anything past him, and you were right. Once, we discovered that some money had been stolen. Scotty said that he would find it that day, and he did. He didn't do it publicly or with any drama, but he discovered the offender, read the riot act (in private) to the soldier involved, and ensured it never happened again. A man of huge integrity, Scotty believed implicitly in the military's high standards. But he upheld them with an unshakable respect for every person's dignity.

Both personally and professionally, Scotty knew what was going on with everyone in our platoon, including me. He was so astute that we all thought he could read our minds. In part, I think that was because he was so fully engaged. He was never just doing a job, getting through the day, or doing what was convenient for him; he was fully, wholeheartedly present.

Among other awards, our platoon eventually won the Brigade Commander's Trophy for athletics—a significant accomplishment, since we were one of only two competing units with female members. And we received a personal visit from the Army Chief of Staff in recognition of the maps we had produced for the invasion of Grenada. I'm proud of what Scotty and I achieved together and deeply grateful for the fun we had accomplishing our goals.

Even after our military paths diverged, Scotty and I never lost touch. Command Sergeant Major Scott, as he became, remained a second father to me until he passed away in 2003, a hidden casualty of war due to his exposure to cancer-causing chemicals during the Gulf War. I spoke at his funeral instead of attending my War College graduation, and put miniature teacups on his grave afterward in a small act of homage.

Before leaving the military after 34 years of service, I served in Iraq and was promoted to full Colonel in the Army, the highest rank attained by a female Corps of Engineers officer at that time. I accomplished that, and all that I've achieved since then, in part because of what Scotty taught me.

Some of those lessons can be briefly summarized: Be fully present and fully engaged. Anticipate and resolve potential points of friction rather than ignoring them. Maintain a positive attitude, hold yourself to the highest standards, and never give up on what you know is important. Those maxims sound simple, but whether in military or civilian life, they are far from easy to translate into action.

Equally important, Scotty's example taught me that there are different types of leaders and different types of strength. You can lead by aggression, intimidation, shaming, and breaking people down. That's a model that many in both the military and civilian world adopt, but there is another choice. You can also lead with conviction, clarity, and trust that others have something to contribute. Your strength can make others feel safe to take risks and be their best; your engagement in what you are doing can inspire others to be just as wholeheartedly involved.

James O. Scott exemplified that kind of leadership and strength. Modeling it for me so early in my career, he helped me become that kind of leader myself. His influence still guides me today, inspiring my more recent work helping others become fully engaged leaders as well. In that work and my life as a whole, I try to pass on the priceless gifts he gave me in a way I hope would make him proud.

DEBRA M. LEWIS graduated from West Point in its first class with women. She is a retired Army Colonel, a Harvard MBA, and a Combat Commander who led a $3 billion engineer construction program in Iraq. Chair of the Hawaii Island Veterans Day Parade, Deb is actively involved in the Hawaii Island Women's Leadership Forum and authored "Decisions Built to Last" in the book *Decisive Women.* Experts at addressing one of the greatest leadership problems in America—lack of employee engagement—Deb and her husband, Doug Adams, help others build stronger relationships and learn to achieve more. Find out more about Deb and her work at www.sunrisealoha.com.

BECKY LOAR

on Gary Miller

I have sung for as long as I can remember. My family has always loved songs and hymns, and the church we attended when I was little had a vibrant youth music program—I adored singing in the choir as well as in the after-school "minstrel company" they organized, which performed for clubs and venues around town. I have always known I would grow up to do something related to music. Having watched many of my peers struggle to figure out who and what they wanted to be, I feel especially fortunate to have had this lifelong sense of calling.

I've also been lucky to have wonderful music teachers and role models over the years; gifted, dedicated people have helped me at every stage of my life, in music and beyond. It's difficult to select among them. But asked to write about just one mentor, I have to choose Gary Miller, my choir teacher in high school and a longtime source of knowledge, guidance and inspiration.

I don't remember my first glimpse of Mr. Miller. He probably came over to our junior high to talk about the high school choral program. He was a little shy of 30 at the time. Of course, to a teen-ager that seemed nearly ancient! He had a beard, mustache, and mullet hairstyle, which are grayer but otherwise mostly unchanged today. He liked to joke that if a student sang well enough, he would cut his mullet. But despite a lot of excellent singing, I have no doubt he'll take that haircut to the grave.

As I learned over time, he had earned his degree in music edu-cation at Appalachian State University in Boone, North Carolina and took his choirs to venues and competitions all around the world in locations as diverse as the Vatican and Carnegie Hall. But personally he is a "country boy" who loves fishing and his farm and has spent most of his life in or near Vero Beach, Florida. Having grown up in a clan in which everyone worked in the family's Vero Beach citrus grove business, I could relate to that.

Once enrolled in Vero Beach High School, I naturally signed up for choir. It was a demanding class that met every day. During the first class sessions I remember thinking that Mr. Miller seemed somewhat intimidating. He has always been a person who doesn't mince words. If he says something, he means it; if he disagrees, he tells you. I appreciate that today but when I was his student it could be a little scary. I worried that he disliked me and I felt like a thorn in his side. Looking back, I know that he appreciated my talent—he just demanded the very best from all of us and didn't waste time on flattery.

Mr. Miller's high expectations, no-nonsense attitude, knowledge of and passion for music all had a profound impact on me. Working under his guidance challenged me and honed my skills. Soloing with our choir when we performed at an international youth festival and competition in Vienna was an amazing experience for a high-school student, and it couldn't have happened without his leadership.

In particular, two pivotal encounters with Mr. Miller changed my life. The first occurred the summer between my junior and senior years of high school. As the choir's soprano soloist I got plenty of attention and praise. The proverbial big fish in a small pond, I didn't yet have an accurate sense of the toughness of the music world beyond my school, church and hometown. Sensing that, one summer day Mr. Miller gave me a reality check that ended with, "When you walk out that door, there are a million like you."

The idea that I was just one singer among many was crushing. I went home and cried more or less nonstop for three days. Yet Mr. Miller was right: competition among vocal performers was fierce and the number of other hopefuls was huge. In being bluntly realistic with me, he did me a tremendous favor. For the first time I faced the difference between being a star in my own small community and becoming a success in the world of music beyond it. My senior year of high school was musically fruitful because, thanks to that conversation, I "bought into" the choral program, my private lessons, and music generally in a new and deeper way. I didn't understand it then, but those words from Mr. Miller helped put me on the path of a true professional rather than just that of a dedicated amateur.

My other most pivotal discussion with Mr. Miller was another reality check. I had been admitted to a summer program called the Aspen Opera Center, part of the Aspen Music Festival and School in Colorado, but then decided not to go. When he found out, Mr. Miller gave me "the look." "Are you nuts?" I remember him asking me. "Why aren't you going?" The girlfriend who had planned to accompany me couldn't go, so I didn't want to either, I explained. I got that look again. Making no bones about it, he told me that this was a priceless opportunity and one I absolutely shouldn't miss.

I listened to his advice. Aspen and the Rockies were gorgeous, it was amazing to be around so many other musicians—and I was totally out of my depth. I did a lot of sitting back and watching what the experienced singers did. I saw in real life what Mr. Miller had told me earlier: the world was full of singers just as talented as I was, if not even more so. But despite its challenges, that summer transformed my perspective on opera and classical music, firing my interest in moving beyond the church and choral singing that were my comfort zones. I returned to Aspen for the following summer's session and, with more grounding by that point, my confidence solidified. Had it not been for Mr. Miller, I wouldn't have attended either of those sessions. More importantly, I doubt I would have gone on to earn my Master of Music degree in Opera Performance, much less to tackle the operatic roles I've embraced over the years.

For the past 13 years, Mr. Miller has been the Director of Choral Activities at the Indian River Charter High School in Vero Beach, where my parents still live. Recently I went to hear their end-of-school-year presentation, the first time I had heard one of his choirs in two decades. He can still get a great sound out of any group and it's still clear that he sees the process as being all about the students, not about him.

He is also the Director of Music Ministries at the First United Methodist Church in Vero, where my parents are members of the congregation. Now that I'm an adult, I appreciate his Christian faith and example as much as his musical expertise. And I'll always remember coming back home from Jacksonville, where I now live, to sing at that church—I believe it was for my grandfather's funeral. As Mr. Miller watched me sing I could see his expression of pride in what I have accomplished. It was an unforgettable moment for me.

I have now been teaching voice, as well as singing professionally, for over twenty years. I pass on the high expectations Mr. Miller had for me to my own students: it's either your best or it's nothing. In recent years Mr. Miller has been kind enough to bring me in to do workshops for his choirs. I will never stop looking up to him, but it's also a pleasure to work with him side-by-side, as a peer in the field we both love.

Had I not met Gary Miller, I'm certain I would still have done something in music. But I'm not sure I would have worked as hard or gone as far as I have. His example and advice have shaped who I am as a musician, a teacher, and a person. If I can pass on to my own students even a small portion of what he has given me, I will count myself very blessed.

BECKY LOAR is a Christian vocal artist who sings to bring the Lord's word to life. A native Floridian, Becky received her B.M. degree in Vocal Performance from Samford University in Alabama and her M.M. degree in Opera Performance from the Manhattan School of Music. Becky has performed with the Aspen Opera Theatre, Bronx Opera, New York Philharmonic and the American Symphony Orchestra, among many other ensembles. An active vocal adjudicator and clinician throughout Florida, Becky currently teaches on the voice faculty at both Jacksonville University and University of North Florida in Jacksonville. Her first CD is *Rise*. Becky resides in Jacksonville, Florida with her husband Victor and their children, Charlotte and Nathaniel. Find out more at www.rebeccaloar.com.

PAT MURPHY MCCLELLAND

on Florynce Kennedy

I was a young woman in New York in the early 1960s, come to Manhattan to make my mark on the new world rising all around me. I had left behind my childhood home full of poverty and deprivation, and had abandoned my religion despite my misgivings about what would become of me in the afterlife.

It was a heady time to be in New York: the close of Eisenhower's post-war reign, with its lingering worship of the militaristic, and the opening of Kennedy's Camelot era. All things were possible if you were tuned in and 22.

In counterpoint to the stifling sameness of the 1950s, culture was exploding every which way. In music, Bob Dylan, not yet 21, was stirring rebellion in the souls of the young, talking the blues and passing the hat at the Gaslight Café in the Village. In film, the edgy, collective dreams of Antonioni, Fellini, and the French New Wave were displacing the worn-out clichés of *Pillow Talk*, *Peyton Place*, and John Wayne's lumbering machismo. Politically, the vanguard issue was civil rights, the harbinger of the peace and feminist movements that were to rattle many complacent bones by the end of the decade.

I was enrolled at New York University, one of several stations on my ten-year pilgrimage toward the degree I hoped would ultimately release me from my Irish-Italian provincialism and the boredom of secretarial life. I worked part-time as an executive assistant to a tri-state lawyers' association for $3.50 an hour. That paid my half of the $95 rent on a glorified coffin of an apartment on the fringe of Spanish Harlem, with just enough money left over to buy opening-night tickets to Lincoln Center's first season.

My boss was a law school dean, an honest republican who took a genial interest in me. He was impressed by my "sand." (That's a wonderful word Mark Twain uses in *Huckleberry Finn* to describe one of his memorable female characters: "There warn't no backdown to her, I judge….in my opinion she had more sand in her than any girl I ever see.") My boss suggested I consider law school and offered to admit me to his program. I gave it some thought, though I had never seen myself as a lawyer. Its appeal? It seemed at the time a shortcut to freedom.

As I vacillated between the pros and cons of a law career, another mentor interceded, fortunately for my greater well-being. Florynce "Flo" Kennedy was a board member of the association for which I worked and a well-known Black activist lawyer. Flo knew the reality of discrimination against women, especially women of color, in the early 1960s. When she applied to Columbia University's law school, she was refused admission. In her 1976 autobiography, *Color Me Flo: My Hard Life and Good Times*, she wrote,

The Associate Dean, Willis Reese, told me I had
been rejected not because I was a Black but because
I was a woman. So I wrote him a letter saying that
whatever the reason was, it felt the same to me,
and some of my more cynical friends thought I had
been discriminated against because I was Black.

One of her cases involved representing the estates of the jazz
greats Billie Holiday and Charlie Parker to recover money owed
them by record companies. She won the cases, but the experience
soured her on the law. An iconic feminist, she is said to be the source
of the wry observation, "A woman without a man is like a fish without
a bicycle." Flo often sported a cowboy hat and pink sunglasses.
Another trademark was false eyelashes, which she referred to as her
"Daffy Duck" lashes.

She was brainy, gutsy, charismatic, and utterly unsentimental. She
took me to lunch in Chinatown one June afternoon. I fell to whining
about how I'd been hobbled by poverty, by my parents' unfulfilled
unconscious wishes, and by all the possibly-preventable vicissitudes
life had bestowed upon me.

Bored by my litany, she tossed the price of our lunch on the table
and eyed me with withering disgust. "I'm ordering you to take the
afternoon off and take a ride with me. Your vision needs some
adjusting."

She hailed a cab and directed the driver to an address above
125th Street. As we rode through the steaming density of Harlem,
she waved at the passing scene and began a good-natured
diatribe.

"I grew up during the Great Depression. My family knew poverty but didn't let it stop us. My parents raised us to believe we could achieve anything we set our hearts and minds to. I moved to this neighborhood in the early 1940s as a young woman with no easy future and nothing to lose by taking risks. This scene is central to my inner landscape. I rebelled against what didn't work for me and prodded the world to behave in ways I could tolerate."

She laughingly ended her riff with, "Go and do likewise."

She was my friend for life at the end of that afternoon. I idolized her savvy; mostly, I cherished her cutting honesty. She took me under her wing, inviting me and my friends to what she called her "black and white" salons on the East Side, raising our consciousness without a trace of pious sermonizing. How I remember those evenings. We all felt so "far out" and hip, hanging with the activist Left in her kitchen, admiring a photo of Charlie Parker blowing his horn into eternity. The major takeaway from Flo and her liberated friends? They moved our parochial twentysomething crowd out of our all-white world into the vibrancy of mixed colors and a taste for difference. And they modeled the meaning of mentoring: the sense that we are all connected and owe it to one another to pass on what we have learned.

When I told Flo about the law school offer, she howled with laughter and said, "Don't you do it, child. The law's no place for a woman, not yet anyway. They'll stick you in a corporate law office doing mind-numbing research and you'll hate it 'til the end of your days. Anyway, you don't have the mind for that kind of law—for any kind of law. I sense you're meant for other things."

I can scarcely imagine better (re)mothering for a young woman reared to revere authority, overvalue male opinion, and drift toward security against her better judgment than the sort Flo bestowed upon me in that era of compelling change.

And I took Flo's words to heart. She was right. I was meant for other things. Many of my choices in later life bear the stamp of what I learned from her.

Following her activist lead, I joined the Peace Corps in 1965. Destiny took me to the Mississippi: a turbulent snake of a river, a mirror of the Deep South as I saw it back then, to Southern University, an all-Black campus in a small town in rural Louisiana, for Peace Corps training, the Kennedy-inspired moral errand of the 1960s. Despite some newly-won progressive leanings, I remained fundamentally clueless about the rules of the game south of the Mason-Dixon Line. And the "strong brown god—sullen, untamed," the venerable Mississippi, would figure largely in my deeply remembered experience of the segregated South at a turning point in its history and in mine.

As the 1960s drew to a close, I opted to attend a radical graduate school, the State University of New York campus at Buffalo, the Berkeley of the East Coast. There I fought for civil rights by engaging in sit-ins and forcing the administration's hand by going on strike. I wrote my thesis on Mark Twain's late novel *Pudd'nhead Wilson*, his striking portrait of the deep, dark roots of slavery.

I mainly write poetry these days—some of the social justice variety, including a recent poem about the Ferguson incidents.

I never saw Flo after I left New York. But she has stayed in my heart and forever turned my head around.

California transplant **PAT MURPHY MCCLELLAND** loves the art of autobiography, memoirs, and personal narrative poetry, which she herself writes. A member of the National Association of Memoir Writers and She Writes, Pat has published several children's books. She has taught creative writing in Los Angeles and also taught "Writing for Healing" at the University of California at San Francisco Comprehensive Cancer Center. Her poetry has appeared in journals including *blynkt, Caravel Literary Arts Journal* (where the poem referenced above appears), *Snapdragon Literary Journal, ARAS Connections: Image and Archetype, Altadena Poetry Review, Feile-Festa Literary Journal,* and *Atlas Poetica;* she is also the author of a chapbook, *Turnings,* and a piece in the anthology *Chronicles of Eve* (Paper Swans Press, 2016). She is currently revising a book-length prose memoir, *The Masks of Grief.* Find out more at www.linkedin.com/in/patricia-mcclelland-53722336.

LYDIA MCGRANAHAN

on Marilyn Bousquin

'Ve backpacked solo, climbed mountains, jumped off cliffs into glacier water, hiked past signs that caution BEAR WARNING: STAY CLOSE TOGETHER AND MAKE NOISE. I wore fearlessness like a badge of phony bravery and bogus self-esteem over my hidden fear and shame.

Beneath the surface, secrets I'd swallowed long ago lodged in my stomach like a handful of obsidian rocks that lanced open a past my younger self—a skinny girl with brown eyes and curiosity—swore she'd never tell. I was holding her secrets. Exposure could kill us.

"You're going to write a book about your life." The first time I heard this voice I was alone in my car. No way! It didn't matter that I believed it was God who spoke to me. I would never tell what happened during the years of my mother's second husband.

But the voice persisted. "You're going to write a book." I ignored it. Hid from it. Ran from it. It ran with me until it woke the girl I once was. Piqued her old curiosity. She lifted her chin high enough that I could see her face. Dried skin flaked from the cracks around her tightly closed lips. Tears as thick as scum water sat stagnant in her eyes. She'd been stuck here for almost thirty years. She both feared exposure and longed to be known. I knew in the pit of my stomach, where memories growled like angry bears, that I had to help her. But how? Maybe a therapist. Maybe medication. Maybe a friend. Maybe another long solo hike where I could let her loose into the wild where she could scream and cry and run beyond BEAR WARNING and never come back. Nothing worked. She couldn't speak.

"Write," the voice said.

I'd never written before. The skinny girl with brown eyes had been forced into the back of a station wagon when she should have been in school. I picked up a pen, grasped it like a heavy ice ax, jabbed it into the mountainside of my past, then froze. I picked the pen up again, tripped and fell, face first, bruised and helpless. I continued to struggle with the pen and my past, tearing up page after page of words that exposed my secrets.

Ten years I tried to write. And ten years I tried to quit. But the voice urged me on: "Write your story."

Writing was a mountain impossible to conquer alone. But how could I give up? Even when the girl with brown eyes was skin and bones, bed sheets tied around her ankles and wrists to hold her down, she didn't give up. I carried her limp body forward to search for help. I Googled "how to write a memoir." One website led to another until I found Writing Women's Lives™. *Who is this Marilyn Bousquin, mentor for women who write about real life?* It appeared that she helped women like me write their story. *Is this what I need? A writing mentor?*

I emailed Marilyn, testing the waters, half a toe in. She asked me to fill out paperwork so she could learn more about me, my story. *Oh no! Oh no-no-no-no-no!* I scrambled backwards as though a grizzly were coming after me, my feet slipping all over the scree. Marilyn said she would love to talk about my writing needs. *Talk? I don't "talk"!*

A shard of obsidian must have bloodied my senses because next thing I knew I'd agreed to a phone call. My hands shook and my heart pounded as I teetered near the cliff. Marilyn's voice remained calm and assured. I slowly backed away from the edge, but I didn't take my focus off her. I'd long since learned that humans, like bears, are harmful when they get too close.

Marilyn believed I was capable of writing a book. My younger self—ever curious—gave a weak nod of approval. So I did the scariest thing I'd ever done in my life. I hired Marilyn as my writing mentor. I didn't know then that I had just turned the corner onto a new trail, set foot onto the path that would change my life forever.

I followed Marilyn, my Sherpa, into bear country. Stomach cramped, hands trembling, chicken skin all over. We stayed close together as she nudged me through the dark. Marilyn saw past the debris that camouflaged my truth on the page. She asked me to unpack the very sentences I swore I'd never tell. With my pen and her support I began to expose the old secrets. I told Marilyn how my mom had turned a blind eye on the abuse, blamed me for it, and then rejected me as her daughter. Marilyn listened to the girl, actually cried for her. She believed I had a voice. *Me? A voice?*

Marilyn taught me how reflection was a way to develop my voice, and how to write in scene and use metaphor to tell my story. I wrote and wrote. When flashbacks struck and memories pounded me to the ground, Marilyn stayed close beside me by phone and email and metaphorically held out a pen. Memory by memory, I wrote. As I wrote, tears and words streamed like waterfalls, cleansing and healing old wounds. Through writing, my senses came alive. Sweet smells of dirt and tree bark, ferns and berries. Vibrant colors I'd never noticed before burst forth from wildflowers I'd seen many times. For the first time, I heard beyond the mass choir of birds singing their collective song; I heard each individual voice.

Listen.

Can you hear the voice of the girl who once feared bears? She and the "me" of the present are sticking together and making noise now, pen in hand. Turns out exposure is freeing my voice and saving my life. My pack has never felt lighter. I owe my freedom to Marilyn. She listened to me first, believed in the curious girl buried in those secrets, encouraged me to write, and loved me. My book is on its way. Listen. Can you hear its noise?

LYDIA MCGRANAHAN lives in Oregon with her family. She's a fitness instructor at a Salvation Army Kroc Community Center and a Level Ten gymnastics judge for the USA Junior Olympic program. She is currently working on a memoir about love, freedom, and bald eagles. Her writing reflects the determination and perseverance of an individual who refused to give up, even against all odds. This essay is her first publication. When she's not writing, she's backpacking in the wilderness with her chocolate Labradoodle.

JOHN MACKIE

on John Gilbert Mackie

John Gilbert Mackie was my father, and he was my mentor. He was the best man I ever knew. John Gilbert was named after his paternal grandfather, who immigrated to the United States in the 1860s, coming from Inverness, a small city in the Highlands of Scotland just above Loch Ness. My father was the third child of Percy Mackie and his wife, Mable. Though not homeless by any means, Percy and Mable were, however, poor. They survived because Percy ground out a meager living as a mechanic fixing things for neighbors—mostly their automobiles—in his rickety backyard garage in Sheepshead Bay, Brooklyn.

Unlike today, poorer families of that era didn't clamor to ensure that all—or any—of their children went on to higher learning, regardless of a given child's potential for academics. Survival was the name of the game. Richer kids stayed in school and went on to be further educated in college and university. My father, like many other intellectually gifted but poorer young people of the era, was forced to leave school—in his case, in the sixth grade—in order to go out to work, learn a trade, and contribute to the family's support and survival. (Please permit me to segue into a brief rant here. Society has now gone full circle. Today, it seems, everybody goes to college, rich or poor, even if many are functionally illiterate, have no knowledge that our government is made up of three branches, and register IQs falling somewhere around forty-below-zero. And… they get a degree. Thank you; end of rant.)

I believe that the trades of that earlier era, from around 1910 through the early 1950s, benefitted tremendously because of people just like my father. Because these people were financially unable to consider pursuing higher education, they instead infused the trades with bright, strong, thirsty and creative minds. It was the age of the true craftsman. That was really true during the Great Depression, at a time when the state of the economy dictated that parts and equipment be disassembled, repaired, and patched together to be kept in service…not simply replaced with costly new.

In my father's case, he was a mechanical genius with an innate understanding of geometry and mechanical theory. Though never a member of the US Navy, he was certified by them in virtually every trade. Over the years, he had achieved the ratings of chief electrician, chief machinist, chief carpenter, as well as chief welder. With his gifted hands, his brilliant mind, and his theoretical insights, there was absolutely nothing he could not do.

Because of his many and diverse skills, when World War II broke out he was selected by the Department of the Navy as superintendent of Sullivan's Shipyard and Dry Dock in Brooklyn, New York. There, he oversaw the round-the-clock, day-to-day operations of the 28,000 men and women who spent the war supplying our Navy with destroyer escort vessels. All this at the tender age of 28.

But my father's talents were not limited to turning wrenches or milling steel to within one-millionth of an inch. Not by a long shot. His even greater talents revolved around his understanding of the world around him and of his fellow man. And that is the real reason he came to be the one-and-only mentor in my life…and, ultimately, my very best friend.

My parents had been separated for years, and I and two younger siblings resided with my mother. Though always available to us for any emergencies, for most of my youth I saw little of my father. He would come by once a week to spend some time with us kids and bring my mother her "house money." He would stick around until the discomfort level raised by mom became unbearable and then leave. He always attended open school nights, and for Christmas and birthdays could be relied upon to be over-the-top generous.

When I reached the age of 16, I suspect my maturity clock had started to run a bit ahead of itself. For starters, I had discovered girls and beer—I don't recall which came first—and I also began hanging around with a tougher crowd. I made some other not-so-wise decisions as well. For example, I came to actually hate high school. I felt like I wasn't learning anything really useful there (I still believe that). Even though I could read, write, and speak the language fluently, my high school English teacher consistently saw fit to flunk me. Although I still do not know a damn dangling participle from a conjugated verb, I went on to author five full-length novels for the publisher now known as The Penguin Group. If only Ms. Marsh could see me now.

Well, anyway: midway through 11th grade, I inveigled my mother to sign off on letting me quit school so I could go out into the world and seek my fortune. I found no fortune. For the next year, I bounced from one dollar-an-hour job to the next. They all sucked. Frustrated at my failure to find half-way decent employment, and seeing myself going nowhere fast—not that I really had anything to offer—I decided to join the Navy and see the world. But when my father got wind of that decision, however, he stepped in…and then my whole life changed.

I went to work at Parade Motors Lincoln & Mercury, where my father was then the general manager. There, he ran the crew of mechanics in the repair shop, oversaw the tin knockers and painters in the body shop, and also dealt directly with all of the service customers. He wrangled with insurance adjusters and claims managers. He maintained and managed the time-consuming warrantee-work account with Ford Motor Company. And he did it all with aplomb. I worked with and for him for the next four years. For me, those four years at Parade Motors equated to acquiring a master's degree from Harvard. For it was there that I got the schooling that I really needed: a nuts and bolts, hands-on education in life.

During those treasured years, I was privileged to watch and learn from this gifted man as he dealt with all sorts of peoples, issues, and problems. In essence, he provided me with real-time lessons in sociology, psychology, business management, and ethics. But mostly he taught me how to read and deal with people. It was a talent that I took with me when I left Parade Motors, and one that served me well throughout my years on the streets with the New York City Police Department. During the time we worked together and over the years thereafter, the father-and-son bond that we shared evolved; we became equals and, ultimately, fast and dear friends who honored each other's thoughts and judgments.

My direction in life was forever changed when my father stepped up and took me, a very at-risk kid, under his wing. I have no idea where life would have led me had I joined the Navy all those years ago. It was simply a path not taken. But under my father's tutelage, I went back to night school, then moved on to college. I had a glorious career in the police department, and then went on to become a published author. None of that would ever have ever happened without his guidance, support, and eternal faith in me.

Basically, when you get right down to it, Dad was just a mechanic. But his knowledge of the ways of the world, and his insights and broadness in thinking, endeared him to so many. To know him truly was to love him. When he died at the absurdly young age of 60, he was widely mourned. The line of cars in the cortege that followed him to the graveyard was longer than any I have ever seen before or since. It must have wound for miles. Those cars were filled with a broad spectrum of the world he knew and loved—people who flat-out admired and adored him. They represented the work-a-day and the high-born. They were the laborers and tradesmen; they were the professionals: the doctors, lawyers, judges, and police chiefs.

And they would all miss him greatly. To this day they all speak of him glowingly. But no one has ever missed him as much as me. He was my father; he was my mentor...and he was my best friend.

Born and raised in Brooklyn, **JOHN MACKIE** grew up imagining himself wearing a Dodger uniform and playing third base. When the fantasy of youth faded into reality, he became a New York City policeman, discovering that he would rather be a New York City cop than a third baseman for any ball club....well, almost. During his 17 years with the NYPD, he was decorated over 30 times and awarded the prestigious Medal of Valor. Since work-related injuries forced him into early retirement, he has published five Thorn Savage novels. John's essay on the inspiration for the series appears in Stories of You Books' *Stories of Inspiration: Mystery Fiction Edition.* John now makes his home in Florida. Find out more at www.mackiej.com.

GLENN MARSCH

on Frederick Peter Guengerich

During the early 1990s when I was a post-doctoral fellow pursuing research in DNA damage and repair, I was in an airport hub somewhere waiting for my connecting flight to attend an American Chemical Society meeting. I saw in our gate area a middle-aged man in keen discussion with a younger woman about a sheaf of papers and a research poster, and I recognized the relationship between a professor and his grad student or postdoc. I said to myself, "That is a serious scientist." I later learned that this was Professor F.P. Guengerich of Vanderbilt University, one of the world's top researchers in the fields of pharmacology and toxicology.

In 1996 I took a physics teaching position at Union University, a liberal arts school in Jackson, Tennessee. I still wanted to do some research, so I sent my résumé to Professor Guengerich. After some correspondence, he invited me to work on a nice, challenging project involving DNA damage instigated by a class of simple chemicals called dihaloalkanes. (Methylene chloride, an industrial solvent, is a member of this class of compounds.) Thus, in 1999 I began one of several summer stints at Vanderbilt, about 120 miles from Union.

I was excited, because I knew of Guengerich's exceptional reputation, though I had not formally met him. My impression from the airport was confirmed when I entered Fred's busy lab and began reading his posted rules for his "lab dogs," as he affectionately called us. *What's this? Fred has more commandments than God!* I remember reading one that said, "I shall do unto you as you do unto the equipment." (I now use that one a lot with my own students!) That litany of commandments was helpful, because Fred gave clear expectations, and we knew what we had to do. That had a way of clearing my psyche and enabling me to get down to the business of science.

I had spent two postdoctoral appointments using a technique called fluorescence spectroscopy to study how DNA is damaged by larger, bulky molecules. Since DNA is the genetic code or the "molecule of life," when DNA is damaged by chemicals, bad mutations—and sometimes cancer—can result. Understanding this damage and its repair was the focus and hope of my research.

Fred gave me the opportunity to learn mass spectrometry to better characterize how DNA was damaged by methylene chloride. "Mass spec" is an extremely powerful analytical tool because it gives the mass (technically mass per unit charge) of molecules and their fragments. If we are trying to find the structure of an unknown molecule and can generate fragments of this molecule, we can ascertain its structure—it's rather like looking at the fragments of a broken piece of pottery and, from that, reconstructing what the intact piece of pottery looked like.

Not only was I able to use that cool technique, but I was able to include two undergraduate students in the research. Together we learned mass spectrometry, and in two papers we were able to show that all four DNA bases, or "letters"—A, T, C, and G—could be damaged by dihaloalkanes or their by-products. It was a great opportunity for these two undergraduate students to work in one of the best toxicology labs on the planet—and for me to do so as well.

As I neared the end of this work in 2004, I forayed into protein spectroscopy and began some preliminary work on enzymes called cytochromes P450, which Fred Guengerich has made famous (and they in turn have made him famous). The cytochromes sound fancy, but think of them as the body's garbage removers. At the risk of over-simplification (since there are 57 cytochromes P450), if a substance introduced into the body isn't a nutrient, a vitamin, or a substance needed for the body's biochemistry, then it's trash and the body needs to get rid of it. Many of these kinds of chemicals are bioactive and toxic. The cytochromes P450 render such chemicals more soluble in blood, so that they can be excreted. Drugs are such molecules, and while they are in the body, perhaps up to several days, they can exert a beneficial biochemistry that heals. But eventually the cytochromes P450 (and a few other enzymes) clean them up and send them out.

Those in the business of discovering and marketing drugs need to know how the cytochromes P450 metabolize any candidate drug molecule. The most important of these is cytochrome P450 3A4, because it metabolizes almost half of all drugs on the market. Fred discovered this enzyme and has done much to understand it. My main project was to use fluorescence spectroscopy to further study a molecule that binds in complex ways to P450 3A4.

I had by the early 2000s moved to Grove City College in Western Pennsylvania. In 2013 the College awarded me a sabbatical to Vanderbilt University. So our family "loaded up the truck and we moved to Tennessee," spending an excellent seven months in an apartment in Nashville so I could work in Fred's lab and further explore the complex little enzyme.

Along with all those who work with Fred, I re-entered the weekly cadence of "skull sessions" (where ours might be cracked if we hadn't produced any results that week!), journal club and group meetings, Current Contents updates, and many medical school seminars offered at Vanderbilt. For all of the precision and intensity of our work, there is humor in Fred's lab as well. For example, the cartoons. Posted on the glass walls and partitions throughout the lab, the cartoons are exemplified in this one: Fred as Godzilla about to devour a hapless grad student/postdoc/visiting researcher: (and I paraphrase) "You messed up your experiment. Now you must pay!" And the wheedling response: "No, no, I promise to do better!" I never did participate in the Dogs vs. Lemmings softball games, but the team names said it all—we worked hard and followed orders. Fred's lab is the Marine Corps of research labs, with a dash of humor, and it's exhilarating.

Fred looks deceptively ordinary but his mind is anything but. I've known other highly intelligent scientists, but none with his drive and suite of managerial skills. His laboratory often contains a dozen-and-a-half researchers, and Fred actively supervises and knows what each one of them is doing. I've always thought that Fred is made of tachyons, hypothetical particles said to be faster than light. Thus, it feels like Fred has answered my questions almost before I've sent the email asking them.

Fred Guengerich has contributed to the fields of pharmacology and toxicology not merely by the huge body of influential papers that he has published but because of the number of people he has mentored who are now important scientists in their own right.

I am of a much humbler stature, but Fred has helped me do something that can get overlooked in the large-scale celebrations of such an eminent career. Fred Guengerich has had countless graduate students and postdoctoral fellows and even a lot of undergrads in his lab. He has directly and indirectly trained 23 undergraduates just through my collaboration with him over almost two decades. The schools in which I have taught are liberal-arts colleges, with little funding available for research. Due to Fred's largesse with time and resources, all those undergraduates were able to perform high-level research that has been a great boon to their careers.

To use a physics metaphor: induce fission in a plutonium nucleus and you get two or three slow neutrons, each of which can split other plutonium nuclei. Then a chain reaction, and BOOM! Think of the number of people Fred has influenced: what we have learned from Fred Guengerich we can then teach to others, who will then mentor others, and so on. The effect is slower than uncontrolled nuclear fission, but I think it's at least as influential, and a lot more beneficial.

Fred is simply an outstanding scientist, the best I have ever worked with. He has always obeyed his vocation with competence, industry, and integrity. By means of the lessons I have learned while working in Fred Guengerich's lab, I hope that I have helped my own students become better researchers themselves, and given them a vision of what is possible in science.

———————————————

GLENN MARSCH has been a Professor of Physics at Grove City College since 2004, collaborating with F.P. Guengerich as a "hidden physicist" in the Department of Biochemistry at Vanderbilt University since 1999. He has a B.S. in Physics from Clemson University and a Ph.D. in Molecular Biophysics from Florida State University. He completed postdoctoral research in Iowa and California and served as Professor of Physics at Union University in Tennessee from 1996 to 2004. Since then he has lived in rural Western Pennsylvania with his wife of 30 years, author Cindy Rinaman Marsch, and they have four grown children. Glenn Marsch enjoys gardening, making wine with the fruit he grows, and photographing the beauties of creation. His work is displayed at www.flickr.com/photos/sphericalbull.

SUSAN MAZZA

on Donna Harris

When I was asked to write about a special mentor, I didn't immediately think of any of my bosses. A boss is charged with ensuring that you serve an organization, where a mentor helps you develop your own best self wherever that may lead you. A key ingredient in a great mentor-mentee relationship is trust, and the confidence that the mentoring isn't a cover for manipulation or self-interest. When someone has power over you, much less flexes it, your self-protective instinct kicks in and you don't feel safe enough to grow. For all of those reasons, being a mentor and being an employer or supervisor are often mutually exclusive roles.

And yet…as I looked back on it, I could see that my first boss, Donna Harris, was also an extraordinary mentor. Her experience, awareness, maturity, and judgment—the whole package of who she was and what she did—helped bring out the best in me and modeled a kind of leadership style that still influences my work today.

In college, an earlier mentor had prepared me to benefit fully from what Donna had to offer. College hadn't really suited my learning style until I met my marketing professor, who had come out of the business world to complete his Ph.D. In addition to getting me excited about marketing, he unleashed my appetite for learning. Suddenly I felt like earning my degree wasn't just about figuring out how to get good grades, but instead about thinking and engaging. It excited me to experience learning that was based on asking questions and exploring possibilities—that inquiry was as much a part of the process of learning as knowing the answers. Studying under my marketing professor helped me see that I didn't want to ever be—couldn't be—somebody who fit into a box or automatically accepted the status quo. I realized that I don't like to learn proscriptively; I much prefer to go on an open-ended voyage of discovery.

True mentorship can only really happen when you're ready to learn from what your mentor has to offer. My experience in that college marketing class honed my understanding of myself and boosted my excitement about learning. I left college primed to absorb all of the lessons the working world had to offer.

On graduation, I accepted the lowest paying job that was offered to me because I sensed that it involved the kind of work I wanted to be doing. It wouldn't be the first time I was told I was crazy for not choosing what seemed to be on paper a better decision. The position was in the financial information systems area of what was then called Prudential Insurance. As the Comptroller's Office liaison with the Information Technology department, we were using what was then state-of-the-art technology and doing very new things.

All of that suited my love for innovation and for exploring what comes next.

Donna Harris, the group's manager, was of medium height, with mid-length brown hair and a professional but understated style. The first thing that impressed me about her was that she didn't treat me like I was a lesser person because I was her junior in rank, age and experience. She didn't draw boundaries around what I could do based on my position, take credit for my work, or try to mold me in her own image. You earned Donna's respect based on your thinking, your work ethic, and your willingness to learn new things and find solutions.

It was fascinating to watch how she dealt with people. Donna brought her sense of humor to everything, and it naturally disarmed tension. She was unassuming, straightforward, and unbelievably smart. Secure in who she was, her confidence extended to others, so that they felt it too.

One corporate culture isn't the same as another. Starting out, you need a guide to all of those unwritten rules. Donna mentored me in navigating Prudential's complex human systems as much as she did its technology systems. The elaborate chains of command and slow decision-making drove me crazy—I didn't see why we couldn't just cut through the red tape, talk to whoever we needed to, and get things *done*. I could tell Donna the truth about what I was feeling. She never judged my energy or impatience, she just helped me channel it effectively. Talking with her, I could figure out the best way to achieve what I wanted to do rather than keep running full tilt into brick walls.

At the start of a task or project, Donna would sit down with me and articulate our goals. Then she would let me go off and do as much as I could. There was such a sense of freedom and collaboration. I felt as if we were walking side by side and creating something together. Working with Donna, I always felt like we were in new and exciting territory. And I always felt more like a partner than a subordinate.

Back then, I took myself way too seriously. I was so afraid to make a mistake. I had a lot of shame in my life that I hadn't processed yet, so I was very hard on myself. Donna sensed that I was my own worst critic. If I was screwing something up or misjudging something, she would tell me clearly but without blame. If I took something more seriously than I should, she would let me know clearly but with compassion. She helped me be less punishing to myself and to lighten up a bit.

I remember that one day, she came to me and said, "Listen, I've got to talk to you about something. Ben thinks that you're angry in meetings a lot."

"I'm not," I answered, puzzled.

"I don't think you are either," she said. "But you're very focused, and you tend to furrow your brow. He thinks you're upset or angry and it makes him uncomfortable."

At first I was baffled. I can't change the fact that I'm naturally intense, and wrinkling my forehead wasn't a conscious choice. But I realized that Donna wasn't coming at it from the point of view of *don't ever do that again*, or *you're failing*, or *you're making me look bad*. She was thinking in terms of win-win strategies, and that's what we found.

At one of our next meetings, I remember saying something like this. "Before we start, I want to own something. I realized that I kind of furrow my forehead a lot. It might look like I'm feeling angry, upset or even negative. I want you to know that's not true. All it means is that I'm thinking deeply." Donna added the idea that every time I wrinkled my brow, someone should do something to make me laugh. After that, my furrowed forehead became something funny rather than something that sucked the air out of a meeting. Ben became more at ease with me. He'd look at me and decide, *oh, she's thinking again.* A situation that could have led to ongoing tension had been promptly resolved.

Donna taught and inspired me in so many ways. She believed that it was her job to help me soar. With her as my boss, I loved working. I was creating something and learning at the same time, and I had the safety necessary to take risks and try new things.

Ultimately, a true mentor shows you how to look in the mirror and discern what you can't otherwise see. She supports you in noticing your blind spots and making different choices without feeling that you need to change the deepest core of who you are. She allows you to get honest with yourself and to look at what is limiting you because she believes in you so much—probably more than you believe in yourself. Donna believed implicitly in me. She didn't try to make me someone else; she helped me understand and work with my most authentic self and the best of what I had to offer.

Today, my work is about motivating and teaching people to unleash their greatness, supporting them in making the biggest difference they can make in the world. In many ways, my writing, speaking and consulting build on ideas that began percolating in my mind all the way back in my time with Donna. I feel tremendously lucky to have had such an inspirational mentor and role model at such an early moment in my career.

In her roles as motivational speaker, leadership coach, master facilitator and business consultant, **SUSAN MAZZA** works with leaders and their organizations to transform their performance from solid to exceptional. CEO of Clarus Works, Founder/Author of Random Acts of Leadership™ and co-author of *The Character-Based Leader* and *Energize Your Leadership,* Susan was named a Top 100 Thought Leader by Trust Across America in 2013 and 2015 and a Top 50 Innovator in Leadership in Inc. in 2016. Susan and her family live in Vero Beach, Florida. To learn more about Susan and her work, visit www.randomactsofleadership.com, which has been named among the Top 100 Leadership Blogs since 2011.

LISA NIRELL

on Diana Nyad

You have a choice. You can determine whether you're going to stay on the shore and lament the water conditions, or dive in and see how far you can go. Which will you choose? Here's some inspiration from Diana Nyad.

It was 1978, and her first attempt to swim from Havana to Florida failed. Over the ensuing decades, battles with jellyfish, salt water-induced skin swelling, sharks, rain squalls, and sunburn remained her enemies after four painful attempts.

Thankfully, those days are far behind Diana Nyad. In September 2013, at age 64, Diana's toes touched the sandy shores of Key West.

Fifty-three hours and 110 miles earlier, some people had their doubts this would really happen. One of my mentors opined that she would fail. Another business colleague declared that her friends in Miami consider Nyad "a little unstable to have wanted to continue to try so many times after almost dying on the last attempt."

These are the common responses when any leader—a high performing athlete, Chief Marketing Officer, business owner, or technology visionary—declares some outrageous goal, and commits their waking moments to reaching it. They polarize groups. That's their job. They build communities of raving fans as well as droves of doubters who stand on the shore.

As I see it, Diana's 35-year project proves that she is a leader. She is shining a light for people who impose limits on their true potential. She also personifies the healing power of swimming, a sport I have enjoyed since I began swimming across Auntie Helen's private lake in Winsted, Connecticut at age nine.

Diana and I first met in 1998 at a fundraiser in Los Angeles. My five minutes with her and Olympian Janet Evans still rank highly on my "most inspiring moments" list.

Today, I think of Diana's persistence and fighting spirit every time I prepare for my next long-distance open-water swim race. Her multi-decade commitment to completing the Havana-to-Florida swim reminds me that I have every reason to be in that chilly lake or rough ocean. The rewards of finishing these races are impossible to measure.

The simple joy of sprinting the final 400 meters of every race towards the shore, knowing that my husband is patiently waiting for me, is enough to keep me returning every year. He always welcomes me with my fleece-lined coat and a kiss. In several long-distance events, I placed first in my age group. I'm not a nationally ranked swimmer or record breaker, nor do I plan to be. I jokingly tell people that, as a 31-year open-water swimming veteran, I am consistently average. But I can still beat many thirty-something women in the 1500- and 3000-meter races. At age 55, I'm okay with that.

As you plan your next goal or project, you have two choices. You can determine whether you're going to stay on the shore and lament the water conditions, or dive in and see how far you can go. If you choose the latter, and it's an unproven course, people will accuse you of being single-minded, irrational, and downright insane. Some people said the same thing about Steve Jobs, Albert Einstein, Sally Ride, Elon Musk, and Diana Nyad. They didn't make history by hanging back, waiting for perfect conditions.

Do you want to put your toe in the water, or do you want to make a big splash?

LISA NIRELL helps CEOs and CMOs accelerate growth and innovation. She's the Chief Energy Officer of *Energize* Growth® and the founder of Marketing Leaders of DC™ and Atlanta. Innovative companies such as Adobe, Gannett, and Hilton hire Lisa to gain fresh insights and launch breakthrough marketing ideas. She is an award-winning *Fast Company, Forbes CMO,* and *Huffington Post* expert blogger. She also authored *EnergizeGrowth NOW: The Marketing Guide to a Wealthy Company and the recently released The Mindful Marketer: How to Stay Present and Profitable in a Data-Driven World.* Download a free chapter and video bonuses at www.themindfulmarketer.com and find out more about Lisa and her work at www.energizegrowth.com.

JAY PARINI

on Alastair Reid

My old mentor Alastair Reid died only two years ago at 88. He was a Scottish poet and translator, and we met him in 1970 in Scotland, where I lived for seven years. He was an astonishing fellow: wry, witty, learned, and lavishly gifted as a poet and critic. My sense of what a poem should "sound like" came from reading him carefully. There was a deep musicality in his work, an accessibility as well, that struck me then and has remained with me throughout my life.

I met Alastair in a pub, having been introduced by a mutual friend. He invited me to bring him poems to read, and I accepted this offer gratefully. I would pedal out to his cottage by the sea in the afternoons, at teatime. We sat in his kitchen, drinking mugs of tea, eating toast and biscuits. He would hunch beside me and silently "correct" my poems, as he put it. He circled words, crossed out lines, rearranged stanzas. Sometimes he would just draw a thick line through the whole poem and push it back to me. I knew exactly what that meant!

Alastair directed my reading as well. (I was not enrolled in any course with him. Indeed, he had nothing to do with the university where I was a graduate student when I met him, in the midst of writing a thesis on Gerard Manley Hopkins and the influence of St. Ignatius Loyola on his poetry.) I had never before heard of Borges or Neruda, but Alastair turned me in the direction of their work, which he was translating. Indeed, he introduced me to both Borges and Neruda themselves—the former came from Argentina to visit Alastair in Scotland. The latter, Neruda, came to London at one point from Paris, and we went to dinner together—a vivid evening for me.

Learning to write was, for me, also learning to read. I remember reading "Among School Children" by Yeats and complaining to Alastair that it was beyond understanding. So he led me stanza by stanza through this complicated poem and its stream-of-conscious movement toward a blazing final stanza where the whole poem focused in the symbol of the chestnut tree, which cannot be separated into leaf, blossom, and bole.

Often I can hear Alastair's voice in my own as I write and read. His accent—a mild Scottish lilt—seems vaguely to undergird my own way of speaking, although only I can notice this. His impeccable ear for the sound of poetry certainly taught me how to listen to a line of verse.

Frost once said that a poem has to carry a tune. I still believe that, and I listen for the tune in any poem. I want to believe its music. I want it to play freshly on my ear. I'm always looking for what Frost famously called "the sound of sense."

In Scotland at that time, there was a kind of poem afoot that Alastair wrote and, perhaps even more sharply, could be found in the work of Norman MacCaig. I met MacCaig through Alastair, and he also became an important figure for me—someone whose work I really cared about, learned from, imitated. In my *New and Collected Poems,* I have a new poem in the manner of MacCaig, although Alastair is there too:

> I take some comfort from old frogs
> who squat around the pond
> like Bodhisatvas, contemplating
> nothing but their own exclusion
> from the world beyond them, falling
> deeper into selfless
> silence and the dereliction
> of all duty but to sit like this,
> apart from offspring
> leaping in the air or falling
> through their parachutes of flesh
> or dying on the road like Jesus,
> with their arms outstretched.
> Articulate composure
> is their mode, as unheroic as
> the rocks around them,
> clumped and cooling as the night comes on.

I can read this poem to myself only in the voice of MacCaig, who had a marvelously whimsical manner. Alastair used to call it "a whim of iron," and that pretty much summed up the case.

As I get older now, moving into my seventh decade, these looming presences from my youth become more important. They played such a role in helping me to shape an image of what poets did, how they did it, and what their poems could do on the page. I think I've spent the past four or more decades working my way toward what I saw then, trying to find and reframe it. In a few poems, I think I've actually got to that point—a kind of arrival that is satisfying. As Eliot wrote so wonderfully in the fifth section of "Little Gidding": "What we call the beginning is often the end / And to make an end is to make a beginning."

JAY PARINI is a poet, novelist, biographer, and critic. His five books of poetry include *Anthracite Country* and *House of Days;* his *New and Collected Poems: 1975-2015* appeared in March 2016 from the Beacon Press. He has written eight novels, including *Benjamin's Crossing, The Apprentice Lover, The Passages of H.M.,* and *The Last Station*—the last made into an Academy Award-nominated film starring Helen Mirren and Christopher Plummer. Parini has written biographies of John Steinbeck, Robert Frost, William Faulkner, and, most recently, Gore Vidal. His nonfiction works include *Jesus: The Human Face of God, Why Poetry Matters,* and *Promised Land: Thirteen Books That Changed America.* Find out more at www.jayparini.com.

ANN PARKER

on Camille Minichino

L ittle did I know when I returned from a vacation early in my work career that the woman I found sitting at *my* desk would end up being one of the most influential women in my life— both friend and mentor.

Camille Minichino was taking a new position at the same scientific research and development facility where I, a shining-eyed newbie fresh out of college, had just started working. Desks being scarce at the time, our mutual boss had plunked Camille in my little flimsy-walled office in the "cooler," where all of us new employees spent time cooling our heels while waiting for required clearances.

Our boss commandeered a second desk and chair, spiffy-quick. Once my ruffled, anxious feathers were smoothed, Camille and I started talking. We quickly discovered strong points of commonality. She had a Ph.D. in physics. I had a B.A. in physics. We both loved chocolate and coffee, a passion that quickly inspired regular morning and afternoon chocolate and coffee breaks. (One or the other of us always had a box of See's Chocolates, ready and waiting, in a desk drawer.) We also both loved books, books, books! (And shopping, at bookstores or elsewhere, but mostly at bookstores.)

Another point of bonding had to do with the fact that the research and development facility where we worked was, at the time, very much a man's world. I can still recall the confusion of folks who couldn't figure out how to categorize either of us. Camille, who was prepping to inspect nuclear reactor control rooms, was as likely to be asked to make photocopies or see to the supplies in the coffee room. As for me, men and women alike were befuddled. Was I a secretary? *Noooo.* Was I a technician? *Noooooo.* As the only female technical editor/writer in the engineering department, I was a bit of a mystery, and somewhat suspect.

Over the years, I have come to appreciate and admire Camille for more than our chocolate-physics-books connection. Camille has the amazing ability to find people of mutual interests and bring them together into book groups, philosophy-discussion groups, Friday-night-movie-watching groups, you name it. She had a natural facility for social networking long before the term meant gazing into a monitor/screen while sitting alone in a darkened room.

Later, Camille was the person who brought me into the world of mystery writing and writers, who set my feet on a "writer's journey." Not that I hadn't been slinging words around with great abandon for quite a while at that point….I had "evolved" from technical editor/writer of engineering specifications to corporate communications specialist to science writer for the well-regarded magazine produced by this very same R&D facility. But fiction writing? Ah, a whole different game. You use basically the same hammer to pound basically the same nails, but with vastly different results.

It all happened as follows:

Camille was always the sort to say, for instance, "Hmmm. I'm going to create a calendar that features important days in science." And she did (mind you, this was *long* before the now-ubiquitous Internet). Then, it was "Hmmm. I'm going to design and sell mugs with scientific people and sayings on them." And she did. So when she said, "Hmmm. I'm going to write a mystery series based on the periodic table, with a female physicist as a protagonist," I had no doubt at all that she would do it.

And she did.

Thus was born the Periodic Table Mysteries series, featuring Gloria Lamerino.

I watched in fascination as Camille went about the business of writing her books, finding a publisher, promoting her books, finding an agent who then found her a *bigger* publisher, writing more, promoting more…

And hey, it kind of looked like fun.

I wondered: Could I, maybe, do this? Write a novel?

When I floated the question, Camille instantly concurred. "Of course you could!"

I demurred. "I need a character. I need a setting."

Camille insisted. "You have a setting. You've been talking about Leadville and its history for a while now. Why not set a mystery there?"

You see, by this time, I had become fascinated with an unknown-to-me-until-then bit of family history: my paternal grandmother had been raised in (of all places) Leadville, Colorado. A "California girl" myself and curious to find out more about Leadville, I did what I did best: started researching a topic which I knew next to nothing about.

Camille persisted. "You have your setting. Now, why not create a female character and put her in Leadville? There were so few women there… She'd be a woman in a man's world!"

Well, hey, yeah. So she would!

Camille prodded. "And you know what that's like."

Well, yeah. I did. And so did Camille.

Encouraged, I took a step onto the road of writing a historical mystery. Camille advised me to take a class in writing mysteries. I took another step and signed up for the class. Then Camille dragged me to a local Mystery Writers of America meeting, and I joined. Another step. And another followed, and another…

Years later, having typed those glorious words THE END for the first time, I knew exactly who to thank for that marvelous, amazing journey, a journey I would have never had either the courage or the will to take all by myself. My mentor, my friend, my chocolate-and-physics-buddy-through-the-decades—Camille.

ANN PARKER earned degrees in physics and English literature before falling into a career as a science writer. The only thing more fun for her than slipping oblique Yeats references into a fluid dynamics article is delving into the past. Her Silver Rush historical mystery series is set in the silver boomtown of Leadville, Colorado in the early 1880s and has been picked as a "Booksellers Favorite" by the Mountains and Plains Independent

Booksellers Association. A member of Mystery Writers of America and Women Writing the West, Ann lives with her husband and an uppity cat near Silicon Valley, whence they have weathered numerous high-tech boom-and-bust cycles. Find Ann online at www.annparker.net.

PETER HAMILTON RAVEN

on G. Ledyard Stebbins

San Francisco was the perfect place for a future botanist to grow up. The Bay area and, beyond it, California offered a magnificent array of natural habitats and species. The city boasted Golden Gate Park and housed the California Academy of Sciences, which was within easy walking distance from my childhood homes. At nine I became an enthusiastic member of the CAS Student Section. Most notable for me was the chance to work with John Thomas Howell, an extraordinary botanist and one whose tutelage and kindness changed my life.

Sponsored by Mr. Howell, I joined the Sierra Club as a junior member in 1948 at the age of 12, the minimum age for membership. (As of this writing, I have been a member this pioneering environmental organization for over 68 years!) In 1950, Mr. Howell was unable to make the Sierra Club's Base Camp trip, which each year brought nature-lovers to a different location in the Sierras and beyond. He asked me to attend in his stead to help fill in further details for his work on the plants of the high Sierra Nevada. At 14,

I was thrilled at the prospect of heading up into the far reaches of the Sierra, seeing what plants might be found there, and helping Mr. Howell with his work.

I was told that a Dr. Stebbins would give me a ride to camp. Making arrangements by telephone, I explained that I would like to bring a plant press with cut pieces of corrugated paper, blotters, and newspaper in order to collect plant specimens on the outing. The voice on the other end of the line responded that he knew what I was talking about and had plenty of room for my press. When my parents dropped me off at his home in Berkeley, I still had no idea who Ledyard Stebbins was. I had been serious about botany for several years by then, but I was just a kid.

As we drove along on our way eastward towards the Sierra, I finally connected the name of one of the plant species that I had been interested in studying, *Hordeum stebbinsii*, with the name of the car's driver. It gradually dawned on me how important Dr. Stebbins was in the field of botany.

Yes, this man certainly knew about plant presses.

He was modest about his own accomplishments, so I had to pry out the details of his activities and professional life over the upcoming days, something I did with relish even though I didn't yet know enough to put it all in context. George Ledyard Stebbins Jr., always known as Ledyard, was the leading evolutionary plant biologist of his time and a figure of the first magnitude in the history of the biological sciences generally. He had earned his Ph.D. at Harvard in 1931, when information about plant chromosomes and their behavior was first being applied to studies of plant evolution. The summer I met him, Dr. Stebbins was making the transition to a new position at the University of California at Davis, where he was to develop and establish a program in genetics. That same year, his magisterial book *Variation and Evolution in Plants* was published to praise from leading lights, including the great evolutionist Theodosius Dobzhansky.

Here was a career botanist juggling intensive research, teaching, academic administration and, of course, a personal life. Yet Ledyard Stebbins extended himself in every way to help me. This may have been because, a generation earlier, he had experienced some of the same things I had. He too had discovered the wonders of the natural world when he was still young; he too had felt out of sync with his classmates, for the identical reason I did—skipping the third grade and ending up younger and smaller than his peers. Whatever his reasons, as we camped and collected together Dr. Stebbins was quick to accept me. He treated me like a peer rather than like a subordinate or worse, a hindrance.

That year's Base Camp visited the upper South Fork of Bishop Creek, on the east side of the Sierra; our camp was located in the green, flowery meadows near the unattractively-named Dingleberry Lake, a small gem of a lake, unbelievably blue, that lay at an elevation of just over 10,200 feet. Naturally, Dr. Stebbins and I both collected plants with great enthusiasm for as many hours as the sun would allow. Once, on Coyote Ridge, I remember darting from one kind of plant to another taking samples and dropping them into the butterfly net I was also using to collect pollinators here and there. Then I delivered the un-pressed plants to Ledyard, my new friend, whom I blithely assumed would press them as his contribution to our joint venture. Not surprisingly, after about two loads, Dr.

Stebbins said "Hey! You take some turns pressing: I want to look at the plants, too!" But he said it with humor, and was unfailingly good-natured with me.

As the days passed, Ledyard began to teach me about the deeper evolutionary relationships between the plants we were seeing. Little as I understood the details of chromosome counts and so on, it was exciting to be involved in his quest for improved understanding. I was making a leap from collecting and learning to recognize individual species to seeing them as parts of an evolutionary and ecological whole. After working beside Dr. Stebbins, I knew enough to ask the core questions: What grows in this region? How does it fit together with other species? What does the whole assemblage of species mean?

Lively evenings by campfire were as much a Base Camp tradition as vigorous daytime activity. Dr. Stebbins was a music lover and a great amateur performer. I remember him introducing and offering his solo rendition of the doleful campfire ballad "Abdul Abulbul Amir." At 14 and a passionate music lover myself, I was probably almost as impressed with Dr. Stebbins's vocal performance as I was with his scientific work.

The end of Base Camp felt like a bit of a letdown, although the ride back home had its own excitement. Dr. Stebbins was known for losing track of everything around him when he was collecting, studying, or in this case, perhaps just thinking about plants. We had a head-on collision while he was driving very slowly down the wrong side of the road. There were no injuries, but the sight of him leaping out of the car and waving his arms in apology and explanation amused me as much as it seemed to frighten the other driver.

Back in San Francisco, Dr. Stebbins stepped into my family's house in the Sea Cliff district to talk with my parents, dropping off the big stack of dried plant specimens we had collected. I had a deep sense of pride listening to this great man tell them about our trip, referring to me as if I were a colleague.

Like that other transformative mentor, John Thomas Howell—who promptly added the specimens I had gathered to the CAS collection—Ledyard Stebbins combined a reverence for plants and the natural world, a rich scientific intelligence, and an innate respect for those younger and as yet less knowledgeable than he was. I have never forgotten their generosity or their willingness to take me seriously, and I have tried to do the same for the younger colleagues I have encountered in turn. No one could have started off with better models of what good mentoring was than the ones Mr. Howell and Dr. Stebbins offered me.

Over the decades to follow, Ledyard Stebbins would introduce me to botanists and other scientists, provide invaluable guidance and dialogue, and accompany me on my first visit to the hallowed halls of the National Academy of Sciences when I was elected to membership 30 years after our first meeting. The friendship that began on that 1950 Base Camp trip lasted the entire remaining half-century of his lifetime, and I'm grateful for it, and him, every day.

DR. PETER HAMILTON RAVEN is a leading botanist and environmentalist and the President Emeritus of the Missouri

Botanical Garden in St. Louis. A frequent speaker on the need for biodiversity and species conservation and one of the individuals named as *TIME Magazine's* Heroes for the Planet in 1999, he is the recipient of the US National Medal of Science, the International Prize for Biology, the Tyler Prize for Environmental Achievement, and a MacArthur Fellowship among many other honors. Born in Shanghai before growing up in California, Dr. Raven has been instrumental in the international project to publish the English-language *Flora of China,* a comprehensive catalogue of China's more than 31,000 species of wild vascular plants that encompasses 22 volumes of text and illustrations.

CHRIS RINAMAN

on Bunky Green

I t was a crisp Florida afternoon in late spring, and I had only a few more responsibilities left in my undergraduate career. I was feeling unburdened because I had finished my senior recital and was glad to be free of the stress of preparing for that and eager to get started on the next chapter of my life. It might seem like a strange coincidence, but it was a natural evolution for me, studying to become a jazz musician without having to really travel more than a few miles from where I grew up—in northeast Florida, of all places. The jazz school at the University of North Florida, the product of the largesse of a grocery magnate, concentrated several talented world-class jazz musicians and educators in my back yard.

The head of the jazz program at the university was the hippest cat in all of Northeast Florida. Vernice "Bunky" Green was an alto saxophone player and a true "musician's musician"—which only made him that much cooler to all the students. Originally from Chicago, Bunky had played and recorded with Charles Mingus among many others, which made him true jazz royalty by association.

During my four years at the school, I had of course heard Bunky perform several times and address the school as a group. He was a presence on campus, so I often passed him in the hall and had small encounters with him in annual juries, but we never really had any significant conversations and I never studied privately with him—that privilege being reserved for the saxophonists, not the trombonists. To me he was a bit like a celebrity—I knew who he was and respected him, but I wasn't sure he really knew who I was.

For my life after my undergraduate years, I had decided that, rather than stay in Florida and perhaps teach band, or move to Orlando and work in the theme park bands, I wanted to go somewhere relevant in the jazz world. I had auditioned for the Manhattan School of Music and was going to move to New York City in the fall.

On this nice spring afternoon, Bunky sought me out. "You busy? Let's go for a walk." Bunky and I couldn't have looked more different. He was always impeccably dressed, usually in a suit and tie, and he looked like a jazz musician! I was a tall, skinny, blond kid from Florida who had never really been away from home. For the next hour we walked and talked and he asked me about my plans.

"So, you're going to NYC?"

We must have talked about keeping up practice habits, or the great music in Manhattan, but I've since forgotten the musical advice. The thing I recall is that after a while he said, "You know, you may meet a lot of great musicians in NYC, people you admire and want to play like and be accepted by. They might be hanging out after a rehearsal or a gig sometime, and somebody might want you to take something, to be a part of the group. I want you to tell them that you're on some medicine, and the doctor says you can't take nothing else!"

That still brings a smile to my face to this day for the sweet and almost quaint tone of the advice, but mainly for the genuine love that Bunky showed me—even if it was a result of his knowledge that NYC was probably gonna eat me alive, this skinny kid from Florida. I'm not sure if this was a standard talk for matriculating students, but I have a feeling he felt I especially needed some of this counsel.

Jazz music, being an aural tradition, is basically only taught and passed on through mentors. I've been fortunate to have had many different kinds of mentors throughout my career. I have had teachers I've spent many hours with—and they have given me invaluable insights and tips on music, practicing and life. Some mentors I've known only through recordings that I've listened to hundreds of times and learned every note of. Some have been colleagues and friends that I know very well and sit next to in bands and orchestras in New York—and work with, and compete for the same jobs with, and socialize with. I've learned from all of them, and I truly value all of them and the incredible insights I've been given. But the way Bunky sought me out and imparted his advice always seems to stand out. Most importantly, his thoughtfulness—that's what really stuck with me over the years.

In my own teaching of younger musicians, I've tried to model that same kind of approach. You can't simply tell somebody what to do or not to do with any real effectiveness, but you can give them a tool they might be able to use, and show them that you care about how and what they do. Bunky embraced what I feel the best musicians, and the best people, know. Success—musical and otherwise—and what you do for a living are important, but the kind of life you lead and the people in that life are the most important.

CHRIS RINAMAN is a freelance trombonist in the New York City area whose performance and recording work encompass jazz, rock, Broadway and classical ensembles. He attended the University of North Florida and the Manhattan School of Music and has toured as lead trombonist and soloist with the Artie Shaw Orchestra and the First National Tours of *In The Heights* and *Memphis* in performances throughout US, Canada and Japan. He also composes, arranges, and orchestrates for vocalists including Deana Martin, Michéal Castaldo, Steven Maglio, and Giada Valenti (in the PBS special *From Venice With Love*). As a former assistant to Academy-Award-winning film composer Howard Shore, Chris was head score consultant for the world premiere of *The Fellowship of the Ring for Symphony Orchestra and Chorus* at the Hollywood Bowl. He has also composed the scores to several independent films and to commercials for Western Union and Staybridge Suites. Learn more about Chris and his work at www.chrisrinaman.com.

ZOYA SCHMUTER

on Werner Spitz

am very pleased to write about my mentor in forensic pathology, Dr. Werner Spitz, who is to my mind the most outstanding professional in the field. I worked with him during my one-year fellowship at Michigan's Wayne County Office of the Chief Medical Examiner from 1985 to 1986, but I followed his career long afterwards.

I graduated from medical school in Gorky, Russia before my family left the then-Soviet Union. Our path took us to Israel and then to the US, where I repeated my medical training. In my last year of residency in pathology at William Beaumont Army Medical Center in El Paso, Texas, I became anxious about finding a job. I mailed many letters offering my services and received answers with assurances that my letters would be kept on file. At first that didn't sound too bad, but soon I understood that this was just a polite form of rejection.

I decided to apply for a forensic pathology fellowship in the Wayne County Medical Examiner's Office, where I had been on the monthly rotation during my last year of residency. That office serves the Detroit area, and not so long ago Detroit possessed a dubious renown as the "murder capital" of the United States. The office was located in downtown Detroit, in a drab painted building that had been constructed before the Detroit riots, and had only poor financial support from the city. However, I was drawn to the expertise of the staff, especially to the renowned Dr. Spitz. He had worked on a number of high profile cases, including the assassinations of John F. Kennedy and Martin Luther King, Jr., and he was the main author of the best forensic pathology textbook in existence, *Spitz and Fisher's Medicolegal Investigation of Death*.

From my résumé Dr. Spitz noticed that I had worked in Israel for Dr. Erich Liban. He offered me a fellowship in part because of his great respect for Professor Liban, with whom he had worked at some point of his career in Israel. The world can be really small! I diligently read Dr. Spitz's entire textbook before starting my fellowship. I had not realized how lucky I was—I felt that he was the top professional in his field. This one-year fellowship was one of the most productive—and in fact delightful—experiences of my professional life.

Dr. Spitz, a German Jew who had landed in Israel after World War II, still spoke with a German accent despite his many years in the US, to which he had emigrated in 1959. He was a noted authority in his field, very active in forensic work beyond our own office, and a talented speaker. He was never afraid to help lawyers understand a case in depth and to educate them for future. Dr. Spitz absolutely did not mind when his coworkers had opinions of their own, even to the point of testifying on the opposing side in a trial—and he enjoyed professional debate, contrary to my experience with many other chief pathologists.

Under Dr. Spitz's leadership, our office's process of examining dead bodies—from the study of all information received from medical investigators, x-rays, and autopsies through follow-up discussions and then on to the final diagnosis—was exceptionally well organized and successful. In a case involving a death from multiple gunshot wounds, for example, I could not find one bullet's exit while performing the autopsy. Coming into the autopsy room, Dr. Spitz noticed the small hole on the heel of one of the victim's feet. *That* was the exit wound. He directed me to investigate the crime scene, and it revealed the important explanation for this unusual finding: the victim was shot while falling from the balcony.

In part because we had both come from backgrounds outside America, I felt at ease with Dr. Spitz, which did not happen with my bosses too often. A few times my husband and I visited his mansion in nearby Grosse Point. I met his mother, an elderly German lady with whom I enjoyed talking. Dr. Spitz's parents had fled the Holocaust by immigrating to Israel. His father was also a medical doctor, and Werner himself had first studied in Geneva and then graduated from Jerusalem University.

In Detroit, I worked tirelessly and strived to learn everything I could from the office and Dr. Spitz. When the year ended, I received an invitation for an interview in the Office of the Chief Medical Examiner (OCME) of New York City. I flew there in July 1986. Elliot M. Gross, the Chief Medical Examiner at that time, knew Dr. Spitz, and that was the best recommendation I could have had. My Russian background was not an obstacle because, as I understood later, several doctors from my country were already working there and the Chief was pleased with their performance. I did not ask many questions; I wanted the position and I got it. Dr. Spitz supported my decision. I took the job in this prestigious and extremely busy office in August 1986, and I worked there for more than 22 years until my retirement.

All those years I followed news about Doctor Spitz in the press. He testified at the criminal trial of Casey Anthony and the civil trial of O.J. Simpson, as well as consulting on the investigation of JonBenet Ramsey's death among many others. I once called him to consult on a case when I had difference of opinion with my boss in New York about whether the manner of death was accidental or natural. He suggested "undetermined" and expressed a rueful opinion: "If you asked four forensic pathologists the same question, they would give four different answers."

Over the years, I sent him my published books. I had written one of them, *Tales of a Forensic Pathologist,* in 2009 to discuss some of my most interesting cases. He phoned me, praising the style as "precise and to-the-point with clear thinking," a great compliment. He said that after more than 20 years of experience in this field I had more than earned the right to share my stories and opinions, and he also mentioned that he too liked the image on the book cover, Rembrandt's "The Anatomy Lesson of Dr. Nicolaes Tulp." He had framed and hung a reproduction of the same painting.

In more recent years, now retired, I was not in contact with him. But in April 2016 I was upset by the unexpected death of my former boss at OCME, who was also recently retired. I started to look on

Google for my mentor, Dr. Spitz. I found a YouTube video with an interview by him…but it was from four years earlier. I nervously called him at his old number in Michigan, not knowing his current situation. When nobody answered, I left a message. How glad I was when I received his return call. He called from his office, where he was working on the new edition of his famous textbook. Speaking with the same energetic accented voice, he said that he was very happy that I had not forgotten him. "I will be 90 in August. Could you believe it?" he asked. I did believe it, and I am very happy that he has had such a long and productive life. I sent him a basket of organic peaches from California's Frog Hollow Farm as a birthday gift.

I am afraid that I do not have enough words and wisdom to describe the greatness of this man. But I *can* say that the chance to work with Dr. Spitz honed my skills and built my self-confidence. If I was good enough to work with him, I knew, I would be good enough to work with anyone else.

ZOYA SCHMUTER, M.D. graduated from medical school in Gorky, Russia. Emigrating from the Soviet Union over 40 years ago, her family went first to Israel, where Dr. Schmuter worked in the pathology department at Israel's Beilinson Hospital. After three and half years, the family settled in the US. As a foreign graduate, Dr. Schmuter again took exams, did a four-year residency and served a one-year fellowship in Michigan. Ultimately settling in New York, she began a career as a medical examiner in the New York City Office of the Chief Medical Examiner. Dr. Schmuter is currently retired and resides with her husband in New York and Florida. Her four books include *Tales of a Forensic Pathologist* and *From Russia with Luck*. Find out more at www.zoyaschmuterbooks.com.

DELIA SEBORA

on Shirley Hagar and Agatha Younger

After three years of night classes, working full time, and with thirty credit hours to go, I quit my job to finish an associate degree. I escaped New York, running from a nun who hated students of color, and from an abusive husband who tried to beat my passion for learning out of me. I ran to my father in Los Angeles, my sixteen-month-old daughter in tow. Ms. Hager and Ms. Younger taught African American Literature and Shakespeare, respectively, at my community college. They resuscitated me, and stood me up so I could reclaim the mind I surely thought I'd lost.

I am 21 years old. On my own in L.A. with my three-year old daughter, I look in the mirror. Honestly, I don't recognize myself. I wear lipstick and comb my hair into a halo-shaped Afro. I wear jump suits and long skirts, and I practice yoga. Asthma doesn't fight me as much here. I am free to discover and understand what to do with that person in the mirror.

At 22, I discover my body. It's a great body, full of curves and waves like the Pacific Ocean at sunset. I re-learn my face, still rarely wear more than lipstick. The newness of my body and face make me curious about the person who occupies them. In English class, Ms. Younger takes my hand and sits me next to her. She teaches Shakespeare. I write poetry again in iambic pentameter and she smiles. I remember that poetry was part of my body before. I remember imitating Smokey Robinson poetically "building castles," remember what that body felt like before Sister What's-her-name yanked my hair and called me names, before that abusive marriage, before being homeless with a child, before Ms. Younger and Ms. Hager led me back to me.

Ms. Younger is smallish, her thinning salt-and-pepper hair is brushed back like text on a page. I look at her face, see her lines, a smile, something unblemished. Maybe she's a spinster, a widow. Maybe she was a nun. I don't care. Sister What's-her-name shrinks. Ms. Younger reads Shakespeare like a thespian; her power defies her petiteness. She asks about imagery and meaning in a passage, I answer; she asks us to critique a passage, I write and re-write, sure that I am her only student. She conducts the prelude to my opening aria, says, "Listen to your voice, you see the notes, you hear the music, don't you, so sing, little bird, and fly away high above it all." With her, I learn to unclamp my own tragedy. Maybe she saw it in the face I was trying to reclaim.

Ms. Hager takes my other hand. In her class, we read Dunbar aloud. I don't recognize my voice when I read, but I read all the same. We read Hughes, Hurston, and Brooks; I write stories again, and more poetry. Our class is full of artists, musicians, poets and writers. They form a group. Ms. Hager is our advisor. I don't talk, just read. "Perform Dunbar," she pushes me, and the poet becomes my voice until I reclaim my own. Ms. Hager says smile more; I try. I am too embarrassed and afraid to tell her that when I smile too much, I always lose something. After class, she teaches me to edit and lay out a student paper. Her quick eyes dart from table to copy to ruler where we measure, cut and paste pieces of student writing, including mine, and faculty writing, including hers. I read Dunbar again and hear my mother laughing as she sings, "Jump back, honey, jump back," that line from a Dunbar poem. I write more poetry, then essays and book and theater reviews.

Ms. Hager gives me other books to read. When I finish the first one, she gives me two, and when I finish two, she gives me four more. We sit, Ms. Hager and I. We talk about books, art, creativity and life. She talks fast, always telling me to write more. She doesn't have children, says she wishes she did. The chain on the door to my hidden narrative eases, just enough for me to say I have a four-year-old child, I am divorced, I want to finish college and become a writer. Ms. Hager maps the way home to words that swirl in my head, to the music of my grandmother singing "God Bless the Child" in her Lena voice, to a place where that ache seeks an egress. Ms. Hager doesn't escape with me. She has a nervous breakdown and cannot teach anymore. I lose her.

Ms. Younger and Ms. Hager remind me to listen to the wind, to the sounds of my own thoughts, to the music in my own ears. They hold me and tell me to breathe deeply and sing; they say I can, they say I should. I begin to recognize myself and find my lift again. When I graduate, Ms. Younger isn't teaching anymore; I cannot find her. Just before graduation and her illness, Ms. Hager autographs a book for me: *When in Doubt, Communicate*. Its opening epigraph says that people "learn to keep their mouths shut, and it's the wrong lesson. When in doubt, communicate…you'll be very successful all the way along the line if you just remember that."

I do remember. I first communicate with myself, filling notebooks and journals with poetry and thoughts. I write love poetry, something that was missing until Ms. Younger and Ms. Hager sang Shakespeare and Dunbar. I create my own arias now, and my grandmother's face, her reddish-bronze tone, smiles in mine from inside the mirror.

We all show up in life with our broken places that need healing. Without my mentors, my healing might have faltered, leaving me voiceless. Now, conducting classrooms with my senses finely tuned by them, I listen for the wandering, untutored voices that I can inspire to sing their own arias.

DELIA SEBORA is a native New Yorker and globetrotter. She teaches comparative literature, oral historiography, and world cultures. Still a ferocious reader, she believes that national and international travel deepen our understanding of ourselves, of being human, and of any books that we may happen to read. Delia has worked as an editor for academic, print and multimedia organizations. She completed graduate studies in California and now lives on the East Coast. She is currently writing a memoir about her insatiable pursuit of understanding, lessons learned and battles fought along the way.

G. LEDYARD STEBBINS

on *Theodosius Dobzhansky*

obody can deny that the leader of the storm of interest in evolutionary theory during the middle of the 20th century was Theodosius Dobzhansky. He was the only scientific evolutionist who combined a thorough knowledge of what was then modern genetics—based on the research and theory exemplified by the research of Thomas Hunt Morgan and his associates—with an extensive knowledge of and deep interest in the forces of evolution that operate in nature. Dobzhansky also was enormously persuasive; like all examples of messianic promotion of a cause, his enthusiasm was contagious.

My own friendship with Doby began during World War II, when he decided to study the inversions in *Drosophila pseudoobscura* and its relatives, using as his headquarters a cabin on the edge of Yosemite National Park in the Sierra Nevada. The cabin was at the disposal of Jens Clausen as part of his grant from the Carnegie Institution. About 1943, I decided that I would visit Clausen there so as to sit at the feet of the great Theodosius Dobzhansky and acquire knowledge necessary for my forthcoming lectures and probably a book. When I arrived, Doby greeted me most cordially, but at the same time I realized that nobody can absorb knowledge by sitting at his feet. When not asleep or eating his meals, Doby was either going from one neighboring tree to another to catch flies for his research or was sorting the flies, making the squash preparations necessary for extracting the salivary chromosomes, examining these preparations, or taking his recreation in his particular way. This was to mount a horse and ride as rapidly as possible in some direction. Any bits of wisdom that I could possibly absorb had to be absorbed either during meals or riding another horse in the same direction as the master. Fortunately, my experience at Cate School made me both interested in and capable of riding with him.

One momentous ride was to a high meadow about five miles away from the cabin. There I found two species of the grasses on which I was working, *Elymus glaucus* and *Sitanion hystrix*, which I could easily tell apart while I was sitting on a horse. In addition the meadow contained a large number of plants that were intermediate with respect to growth habit and could be hybrids. I therefore allowed my horse to munch at the grasses in which he had a different but avid interest, while I, without dismounting, picked a flowering head of *Elymus*, one of *Sitanion*, and a probable hybrid. After picking apart the spikelets of the flowering heads, I verified on the basis of both the floral characteristics and the presence of fertility in the species and probable sterility in the hybrids that the meadow in fact contained a large hybrid swarm. I then rode up to Doby, who was also resting in the saddle, and explained my story to him. His eyes glowed with excitement.

"Stebbins, you have made a great discovery," he said. "You are the first person who has seen, collected, and identified a hybrid between species from the back of a horse."

Coming from one of the world's leading geneticists who, in a previous summer in his native land, had ridden more than 4,000 kilometers (about 2,500 miles) on horseback while investigating the ancestry of the domestic horse, this was truly a compliment.

Later on, I decided that I would kill two birds with one stone by demonstrating to Dobzhansky how great was the sterility of these hybrids and finding out myself whether they ever set seed. I therefore went back to Berkeley but returned to the cabin shortly before Doby went back to New York. At that late-season date, the *Sitanion* plants had all matured their seed and were easily recognizable to anybody, as well as being largely knocked over. The *Elymus* plants retained some seed, but were also easily recognized by the short and straight awns on their spikelets. The hybrids were easily distinguished by their shorter stature and longer awns on their spikelets. I therefore asked Doby to gather as many fruiting heads of hybrids as he could and put them in a bag that I presented to him, so that later he could sift through them to search for any seeds they might bear. I promised him a bottle of beer for every seed he could find.

At this he remarked, "You're a piker, Ledyard. When I was in Mexico with Michael White, he wanted to have females of a rare mantid insect that he was studying the chromosomes of. He promised me a bottle of champagne for every mantid."

I was still of the belief that he would find so few seeds that I became magnanimous and replied grandly, "All right, it's a bottle of champagne for each seed."

At this, Doby enlisted his daughter Sophie to help him and together they filled my bag with seed heads. After we had returned to the cabin, they spread the material out and searched. They finally came up with 25 seeds after having looked at several hundred seed heads which, if as fully fertile as the parents, would yield between 50 and 100 seeds. I was dismayed but I stuck to my bargain. Fortunately Doby and Sophie agreed that they could not drink that much champagne. Nevertheless, during the fall of 1946 we did have a champagne party to honor the event.

In 1946, I traveled to New York, was cordially greeted by Doby, and began with him one of the most fruitful collaborations of my life. He absolutely insisted that I live with him, his wife, Natasha, and his daughter, Sophie, in their apartment for my entire three-month stay in New York. My intimacy with this eminent and highly intellectual family I still regard as one of the high points of my life.

In 1969, both the then-Chairman of the University of California at Davis Department of Genetics, Bob Allard, and I received word that Doby was about to retire from his position at the Rockefeller University in New York. Although he was given an option to remain as a retiree, he would no longer be supplied with a laboratory, and his close assistant, Francisco Ayala, would have to go elsewhere. Furthermore, Dobzhansky had just lost his wife, so if he stayed in New York, he would be relatively lonely, as he had not become close to scientists at Rockefeller. Allard made informal advances to Doby and learned that if we could have both him and Ayala appointed, they would both come to us. However, before Doby could come to us on a permanent basis, many arrangements had to be made. I realized that this would be a fine opportunity for me to repay the hospitality that Doby and Natasha had given me in 1946 at their New York apartment. I asked my wife Barbara if Doby could stay during this period in a spare room in our large house, and she assented. I had qualms about doing this because both Barbara and Doby were rather particular and I didn't know how well they would get along together. However, I needn't have worried.

During the spring of 1970, Doby won the favor of our graduate students and his lectures were a great success. He was very much indebted to Barbara for her hospitality, and they had in common an interest in classical art and opera. One afternoon while we were walking to the campus, Doby said, "I want to do something very nice for Barbara because she has done so much for me."

I thought for a moment, then ventured, "She would be delighted with a well-illustrated gift volume of classical art."

"That wouldn't be good enough," Doby responded. "I would like to get her something she can use and enjoy every day."

I thought a little further and then said, "We have a cabin in Wright's Lake in the Sierra. Barbara would very much like to have a canoe that we could paddle on the lake."

"Excellent!" he said. "You order the canoe. I give it to her." I borrowed a catalogue from a friend and picked out one that would be appropriate. Unfortunately, Doby had to leave for New York before it arrived but nevertheless showed Barbara a picture of it, and it was at our cabin by the time he got back in September. We were debating as to what we were to name it, and Barbara strongly recommended that we name it "Doby." I asked him if he would accept that proposal even if it resulted in our telling each other many times while there, "Let's go out and paddle Doby." He said yes, of course.

Born in 1906, **G. LEDYARD STEBBINS** is widely regarded as one of the most influential evolutionary biologists of the twentieth century. His opus, *Variation and Evolution in Plants* (1950), is perhaps the best known among his seven books and other major scientific contributions and provided the conceptual framework for the emerging field of plant evolutionary biology. Stebbins' influence extended beyond botany, and with many colleagues he would fundamentally shape modern genetics and Darwin's theory of natural selection toward what is now acknowledged as the modern evolutionary synthesis. The material above is excerpted from his autobiography *The Ladyslipper and I*, which was edited after his death in 2000 and published by the Missouri Botanical Press in 2007.

LAURA STEWARD

on Barbara Steward

My 53 years of life are richer because of my mentors. Some came into my life for moments, some for a lifetime. My definition of a mentor is someone who transforms who I am and how I achieve my goals—someone who can irrevocably shift my thinking. While most of my mentors are real people, some have come from books and even movies and television. What matters is not where my mentor came from as much as the lesson and how it changes my course.

As I reflected back on my life to consider my greatest mentor, one person kept coming to mind over and over again. You may think it trite when you hear this is my mom, yet I am curious whether you'll still think that at the end of this story.

I was six years old and starting first grade. I wanted to learn to read so badly I could almost taste it. Nothing mattered more to me than finally being able to devour an entire book by myself. Yet when class started, I was told I was not going to learn to read—at least that is what I heard. So I left school in the middle of the day and walked a mile home. Walking out of school was pretty easy to get away with then—not so easy to do now.

Mom was on the phone with someone from the school when I got home. Of course she packed me in the car and took me straight back to school, where I was met by Mrs. Feit and Mrs. Steinmetz, my teacher and the principal. Yup, I remember their names. I can still pull a picture up in my mind of my mom's face when I showed up at home (she wasn't really surprised), the drive back to school as she asked with a Mona Lisa smile on her face why I had left the classroom, and the school officials looking all confused while the three of them were talking at once and then finally asking me questions.

Mom asked the school officials why they weren't going to teach me to read. Of course I had gotten it wrong, they hastened to explain. They were, just not that day. My last name started with an "S," so it would take a few days or more until my turn came. Some moms might have ended the conversation there and said, "Okay." Not my mom.

What I remember most from that meeting was my mom challenging them to consider the policy by asking them, "Why?" Why did the policy have to stay that way when it was so obvious I had a passion for learning?

Eventually the real answer of why they had to stick to the policy surfaced: "We've always done it that way." Mom asked them to consider changing the policy for me based on the fact I was willing to leave school to find someone to teach me. In the end, they moved me up in the list and taught me to read immediately. My passion for reading and asking questions has never waned.

What I learned was a lesson that would stay with me and affect everything I said, did, or even thought from that point on. The lesson? There were actually two: First, the right questions can change your life. Second, "Why?" is one of the most powerful questions you can ask.

Let me explain why. See, I love that question!

When you ask the right questions—and I mean the questions that get you the answers you need, not just the answers you want—life goes in directions you might not have foreseen. People and opportunities come in and continue to shift your perceptions about truth. By choosing the answer that makes you feel a bit uncomfortable, you are stretching yourself outside your current perceptions.

I also learned to listen when I'm on the receiving end of a "why" question. A lot of people avoid a "why" question because it puts them on the defensive. Think about the last time someone asked you why. How did you respond? Did you try to justify the reasons behind your actions, as they did at my grammar school? Once you got to the real "why," did it still make sense to keep doing things the way you were doing them? Were you open to change?

As a mentor, my mom showed me—not just that day, but my whole life, even today—that you need to get past defensive answers and look for real reasons. Not only when you ask questions of others, but more importantly when you ask questions of yourself. I recommend asking yourself, "Why?" five times in a row. By the fifth time, you will have unlocked the real "why" because the first few are most often reflex or defensive answers.

If my mom had ended the meeting after the answer of, "That is the way we have always done it," I doubt I would have founded and sold a highly successful technology services company, written an international bestselling book, or ended up being on broadcast radio. I doubt I'd be writing this today.

Why don't I think so? Because that short meeting when my mom held court shaped my views about giving up, giving in, and going along with the status quo. I learned that my perceptions of a situation are not always accurate. My perceptions are based on the facts I know, and those facts are shaped by the facts others know. Those perceptions are also based on something besides facts. They are based on experiences.

I am not just talking about a parent teaching us that fire can burn or coals are hot. That's a good lesson for life in general, but sometimes it is okay to walk on hot coals. (I know, because I did it in the 1980s at a Tony Robbins seminar.) I am talking about how one person's experiences can create a barrier to growth if you choose to allow that to happen.

When I was going to start my first business, my normally supportive parents tried to convince me not to do it. I asked myself why they were responding negatively and realized they were born during the Depression. Back then, you simply did not leave a secure job without being certain the next thing you did would be successful. If I had made my decision from their perspective, I never would have started my own company. I did use some of their questions to flesh out my plans better, though!

The best way to remove the barrier is to ask questions of yourself and others. And, of course, to read! But you know that last part already, because you are reading this book.

Today my mom has dementia, and we live together. I now ask "why" a lot to God and mom's doctors. As her brain changes, I have to learn new questions, as does she. We both have to think differently about each other, and I am learning sometimes to stop asking questions and just be. Often the answers to my questions are ones I don't want to hear right now.

My mom is still my most valuable mentor and continues to teach me something new each day. There is nothing better than hugging each other every night as we head off to bed. In the moment that we hug I silently ask not "why" but the question I most fear: "Will she be here tomorrow for me to hug?"

LAURA STEWARD is a sought-after speaker, business advisor, radio host and author. After building and selling her highly successful technology services company she started Wisdom Learned, LLC, a company dedicated to educating leaders based on experience and wisdom learned in the trenches. Steward is the author of the award-winning #1 international bestselling book *What Would a Wise Woman Do? Questions to Ask Along the Way*, which was on the Amazon Women & Business bestseller list for over 90 weeks and continues to hit bestseller lists around the world. Through her weekly broadcast radio show, *It's All About the Questions*, keynote speeches, books, seminars, training and one-one sessions, Laura's mission is clear: help people get off autopilot and create amazing, successful lives. Find Laura online at www.laurasteward.com.

CATHY TRUEHART

on Bettie Kravitz

I n the poem I wrote for my mentor, Bettie Kravitz, I called her "mother to many, mentor to more." I could add a long string of other words—inspiration, role model, friend, teacher, guide, soul sister—and still not manage to encompass all that she is to me.

For her 90th birthday this year, she had one of her signature birthday gatherings. There must have been 100 of us together in the elegant restaurant: friends and family and the "spiritual children" she's welcomed into her circle. Reunited regularly at her parties, we've all gotten to know each other over the years, and feel like one big family. At all of her gatherings, guests are given a gift of 18 of something, from 18 wise sayings to 18 new pennies—consistent with the Jewish tradition, the number 18 means "blessed life." What a joyous experience to eat an exquisite meal, enjoy great company, and share in a celebration of Bettie's extraordinary life.

Bettie and I agree about where and when we met but we each have a different story about how it happened. We know that it was at a management workshop being held at what was then called the Amherst Nursing Home (now the Center for Extended Care at Amherst) back in the years when I was working at another nursing home as the education nurse. When I arrived at the adult day care room where the workshop was being given my first impression was that it was gorgeous: modern, full of windows and light, a beautiful and soulful place to be rather than a drab institutional setting. When we were served lunch after the inspiring program, we got the same food the residents ate—and it was like eating at a 5-star restaurant. Everything about that day was so nurturing, so energizing. I recall saying something like, "Wow, this is so progressive. I really need to meet the person who created this amazing place!" With that I was introduced to Bettie Kravitz.

Bettie's version of the story is that she was sitting there, just observing things, when she noticed me because I was the "brightest star" of everyone at the workshop. The way she tells it, she sought me out and introduced herself to me. We tease each other about who's right, but the truth is that it doesn't really matter. We're kindred spirits, each of us knew we wanted to meet the other, and we're still close 30 years later.

Bettie was already almost 60 by the time we met. She had grown up in Pittsfield, Massachusetts and later worked in New York City as a nurse. Later, she started the Amherst Nursing Home, building it from scratch and putting such love and consciousness into every detail. Her husband died and left her with three small children to raise, yet she kept the business going. Operating a nursing home successfully is hard even if you're not a woman alone with young

kids, but she did it. I'm always so inspired by her vision and persistence. Once she sets a goal she stays with it, and she does everything with clear intention and total gusto.

Right from the start I loved her energy and style. She dressed in
vibrant, colorful clothing with long skirts and lots of jewelry. Her
signature was and is her bright red hair. (She still goes to the beauty
salon every week to keep it that way!) She radiates a willing, adven-
turous spirit. I can call and invite her to do something with me at a
moment's notice and she'll get right in the car. Today she's 90 and
has Parkinson's, but even though it's hard for her to get around, she'll
come to anything I ask her to and be delighted to be there. To be
around her vibrant energy is to feel more alive.

Bettie and I are both spiritual seekers who draw inspiration and
insight from many traditions. Bettie is Jewish; I first experienced the
Shabbat blessing and the Passover Seder with her, experiences that
deeply moved me. But she has the same kind of eclectic perspective
I do. She's interested in Native American spirituality, Eastern religions,
and metaphysics as well as Judaism. She prays and also believes in
intuition and synchronicity. Her faith isn't about boundaries; it em-
braces all.

Bettie never hides her spirituality or her faith in G-d—consistent
with a Judaic tradition, she omits the "o" out of respect. She would
no more think to conceal that part of herself than she would try to
change anyone else's beliefs. Her favorite saying is a wholehearted,
zesty "Put it in G-d's hands, honey!" It's her way of expressing her
trust in the divine, her sense that we can rely on a power greater than
ourselves. I never tire of hearing her say that; it comes straight from
her heart and soul. I know that I can go to her with any worry or

concern and that I am always in her prayers. Helping me learn to put my struggles "in G-d's hands," to release my worry and control and need to save the world single-handedly, is her greatest gift to me.

Bettie doesn't just repeat that saying, she lives it. I was powerfully reminded of that during my forties, when her nursing home was building a new Alzheimer's unit. Having always hoped that we could work together, she invited me to become its director. I gladly agreed, but for reasons that had nothing to do with Bettie herself it was a terrible fit for me. I worked myself up into a state of real misery and depression. Leaving that job was one of the hardest things I've ever done.

I ended up resigning abruptly, without the usual several weeks' notice. Bettie immediately sent me flowers and a beautiful letter saying, "I hope you're okay, honey. I'm so sorry." When she would call to see how I was doing afterward, she was never angry or sad about what had happened, even though it must have difficult for her. I think she had put the nursing home, the Alzheimer's unit, and both of us "in G-d's hands." She trusted that it would all work out the way it was supposed to, and it did.

As I mentioned, Bettie has hundreds of friends. She calls some of us her spiritual children. I like to think that I'm her favorite, but I'm sure all of us feel that! She has this immense ability to make people feel special. Even though we both refer to her playfully as my "favorite Jewish mother" and there's a 25-year age difference between us, I always feel that we have an equal, reciprocal bond. She's a mother to me in the sense of an earth mother, a matriarch to this big tribe of spiritual children, someone who makes others feel protected and loved.

As more young people come into my life who see *me* as a spiritual mother or sister, I feel such gratitude for the wisdom Bettie has given me to pass on to the next generation. Her friendship, support and inspiration are such profound gifts, and it's a privilege to give to others some of what she has given to me.

I keep a special picture of Bettie on the altar in my meditation room. In it, three women are holding hands: Bettie, myself and my mother, who at 89 has been my role model for parenting with love and aging gracefully. We're standing in the heart of the labyrinth I created in my back yard. The labyrinth's curves are such a perfect metaphor for the way we have journeyed together through the decades, moving first in one direction and then another but always sharing the path toward our center. Somewhere beyond the frame of the photograph is Bettie's walker, necessary to help her navigate the labyrinth's stone walkways safely. But in the picture our spirits are unfettered, dancing together strong and free.

———

CATHY TRUEHART earned her diploma in nursing from the Worcester City Hospital School of Nursing, her B.S.N. in Public Health Nursing from Sonoma State University and her M.A. in Counseling Psychology from Leslie College in Massachusetts. Cathy has also completed certification programs in holistic nursing, Neuro-Linguistic Programming, reflexology and Reiki. Her book, *The Miracle of Hospice*, shares the insights and memories she gathered over many years as a hospice nurse.

Recently retired from hospice work to care for and spend time with her mother Olive, Cathy lives with her husband Richard and Olive in Southampton, Massachusetts.

REBECCA TYNDALL

on J.K. Rowling

t is a universal fear among hardcover-, paperback-, and e-book readers alike that one day, when the stars align and the unimaginable has happened, we will be able to meet our all-time favorite author in the world and…our dreams will be crushed.

In this nightmare scenario, the harsh reality hits like a Mack Truck and we come to the realization that our role model, the creator of worlds that have brought us such comfort, is mundane. Someone who leaves a 5% tip on lunch. Someone who barks at their child for no better reason than, say, a slight headache.

It is a universal fear that we will feel as Hazel Grace felt when she met Peter Van Houten in John Green's *The Fault in Our Stars.*

Thankfully, I can say that I've never had this experience with any of the authors I have been lucky enough to meet in person. Although I have wondered whether this would be the case with my idol, my inspiration, and my Queen, Ms. J.K. Rowling, author of the best-selling Harry Potter books. ("Queen" is the title the Harry Potter fandom has bestowed upon Her Majesty, so please don't shoot the messenger. If you're not into royalty, we also call her just "Jo.")

There is a part of me that wonders whether I'll ever have the rare opportunity to even be in the same room as her, let alone speak a word. If that ever happens, will I leave disappointed, knowing that this woman I've built up in my head for the past 16 years is but a person made of flesh and bone? Or will she be just as wonderful, just as extraordinary, and just as otherworldly as I've imagined?

All of this is wondering. *"What if?"*

I don't know what that day will be like, because it hasn't happened yet. Dare I say, "may never happen"?

I only know that as I've gotten older, my appreciation of J.K. Rowling has evolved from admiring her and her creation of the Harry Potter universe to admiring her as a person. Thanks to today's new technology, social networking, and access to news right at our fingertips, I've learned enough to appreciate her not only as a fantastic writer and a genius in creating a world so detailed and flawless, but also as a remarkable person altogether.

She is human, yes. She will have off-days like the rest of us, and she will make mistakes as we all have, but I can say in all certainty that I could never be disappointed in her.

Football players who have a dark history, family members who let you down, teachers who made an impact on you when you were a child but who turn out to be just as flawed as the rest of us: I think the problem with people idolizing their role models too much comes from putting all of our eggs in one basket and expecting both the basket and the eggs to be totally perfect.

That expectation is our own responsibility as much as our hero's. The trick is to not look at your role model as a godlike person. Do not erect a statue in the town square, do not assume that their life is more perfect than anyone else's; just look at them as a human. Look in their eyes as though you were a parent. See them as you might see a rebellious teenager, who can make mistakes and still be wonderful, adorable, and lovable.

When you have someone to look up to who's constantly in the spotlight, look at them as a flesh and bone person first, and then begin to appreciate who they are, deep down in their heart.

Now, I would be lying if I said this is how I came to adore J.K. Rowling. Like just about everyone else my age—so-called "millennials" or members of "Generation Z"—I was a fan of Harry Potter and of course, started to devote my life to all things magic. For the longest time, the actual person behind the series was barely a "blip" on my personal radar screen.

Until…

Until I found out that J.K. Rowling donated a portion of the money she made from Harry to charities. Until I knew she named a character in one of her books after a fan who passed away from cancer. Until I knew that she was existing on government benefits when she had the courage to write the first Harry book.

Then I knew what a remarkable person she was. Then I knew that she was more than a person—she was an angel, someone put on this earth for kids to look up to. Because of these things, she makes me want to become a better person.

I fell in love with Harry as a child, and I fell in love with Jo as an adult.

It's entirely possible to fall in love with something—an idea, a person, a prospect—then be crushed at what is revealed behind the curtain. Dorothy went through it, as we all know, and there is always the fear that someday, the thing that we admire or adore most will be our biggest disappointment or even our downfall.

But I think I've chosen a good person to add to the obvious role models in my life, like my parents, the friends who have helped me grow up, and the other authors who were influential in creating my love of reading.

Through Harry, J.K. Rowling has taught me (and many others) about love, friendship, strength, and the power of sacrifices, reassuring me that good will always conquer evil. Through her own example, she taught me that it's okay to have flaws and just as okay to be sad. She reminds me that each and every one of us here on earth, is an important part of life. She taught me never to give up. She taught me to dream.

The most important people in my life are those who have made the largest impact on my journey to becoming who I am today. Even if I never meet her, that most certainly includes the woman, the mind, and the face behind Mr. Harry Potter of Number Four Privet Drive, the Queen herself, Joanne K. "Jo" Rowling.

REBECCA TYNDALL developed her love of reading over 21 wonderful, literature-filled years. At the age of 17, she decided to let her outspoken opinions of books be heard, and launched a blog called *The Literary Connoisseur.* There, she speaks freely about books she loves, books that she doesn't love, books that have impacted her life, and books that have changed her world. Follow her ramblings on www.theliteraryconnoisseur.com and at The Literary Connoisseur on Facebook.

EDWARD O. WILSON

on William L. Brown

I knew him for 50 years, and I've never met anyone else remotely like him. Bill Brown was unique, and I don't think we'll ever see his like again, not just for the rareness of his character, but for the uniqueness of the time in which he lived and worked on his beloved ants. I've thought a lot about what made Bill different, what caused him to burn with such a pure inner light, and I've come up with this: the devotion to his art. His art. He was a scientist to the bone, a hard-core factual investigator, relentless for more information, skeptical in mood, all those things and yet…myrmecology, the study of ants, was an art form to him. It was the center of his creative life, and he was a very creative man. The passion he radiated about this subject turned younger people (we all seemed younger than Uncle Bill) into acolytes, into apprentices; and there was no prize the academic world could offer us more than a rare, measured compliment from the master, something like, "Yeah, that's pretty good; that's really interesting."

I first met Bill through correspondence in 1947, when I was 18, and had already taken my vows, so to speak, in ant taxonomy, just as he had been in contact with *his* mentor, William S. (Bill) Creighton, since he was 16. In natural history, addiction occurs early. In the summer of 1950, I rode a Greyhound bus all the way from Mobile, Alabama, to Boston, and stayed with Bill and Doris in their little apartment near Harvard, as they prepared to leave for Australia and momentous field research in that still myrmecologically under-explored continent. We worked in the Harvard Museum of Comparative Zoology ant collection together, and he gave me the kind of plain, sincere egalitarian treatment he was to bestow on dozens of other students in his field in the decades to follow. He welcomed you, he treated you with respect, he stood in awe with you before the intricacy of the subject, he gladly taught and learned, he created a sense that here in this little discipline was something—to borrow from F. Scott Fitzgerald, the kind of writer Bill so admired—something commensurate with man's capacity for wonder.

In 1950, he was 28 and I was 21, and the whole world seemed ours to possess.

Off he went to Australia, and in the years to follow to just about every other place in the world where interesting ants are to be found, and he was often the first to do serious collecting there. In time he became one of the most widely traveled naturalists of all time, bar none.

He was a key transitional figure in the history of myrmecology. From 1937, when William Morton Wheeler died, into the 1960s, there were very few researchers working on the classification and ecology of ants, and Bill carried the torch to close the gap. For the biologists among us: he played a major role in changing ant systematics from a thicket of trinomials and quadrinomials into a consistent binomial system based on the modem biological species concept. He was the first to recognize the major phyletic division of the myrmecioid and poneroid subfamily groups. He made judicious rearrangements of genera and tribes, "sank" innumerable worthless names into synonymy, and crafted clear, precise revisions widely through the Formicidae and most especially in his favorite groups, the Dacetonini and Ponerinae.

His open, supportive nature drew young people in, and he played a major role in starting the current boom times in which hundreds are engaged in myrmecology around the world. We have truly followed in his footsteps.

Bill Brown was a working-class guy with a first-class mind and a noble heart. He had steel-hard integrity and his generosity to others knew no bounds. He hated a phony, to use one of his favorite words, could smell one a city block away, and put currency in only two things: solid accomplishment and integrity of purpose and representation. He never looked down on anybody socially and he never looked up to anybody. He was unimpressed by rank and status. He never played academic politics, never sought academic recognition or status, but instead waved aside compliments and put others first in research collaboration; he was a righteous man to the inner core.

Toward the end of his life we used to talk about his dream field trip: get into a rich rain forest, sit at a table with a pan and collecting materials, and have graduate students scour the surrounding woods for ant nests which they bring to him to sort, study, and preserve. Dig through some of the "juicy red logs" where ant diversity peaks.

In March 1987, while he was still sufficiently vigorous, I invited him along on a field trip to La Selva, the Organization for Tropical Studies station in Costa Rica. I sat him down on a field chair with a table in front of him, and I was the graduate student, hustling the ant nests for him to go through; and we talked incessantly about the treasures we found. It was a glorious three days.

In his later years Bill filled the same role in myrmecology, and among his wider circle of students and admirers, as the grizzly bear plays in the conservation movement. You didn't see him very often, and some younger researchers never did, but it made you feel good just to know he was there. It made things seem right. Now that he's gone, a big gap has been opened up in our consciousness that will never be completely closed.

Regarded as one of the world's preeminent biologists and naturalists, **EDWARD O. WILSON** grew up in south Alabama and the Florida Panhandle, where he spent his boyhood exploring the region's forests and swamps, collecting snakes, butterflies, and ants—the latter to become his lifelong specialty. The author of more than 20 books, including the Pulitzer Prize-winning *The Ants* and *The Naturalist* as well as his first novel, *Anthill*, Wilson is University Research Professor Emeritus at Harvard and makes his home in Lexington, Massachusetts. Find out more about Wilson and his work at www.eowilsonfoundation.org.

BOB ZIELSDORF

on Burnell Roberts

The familiar saying "beware of what you ask for" suggests that asking for something you want can be dangerous. That's probably true at times. But one of the times I did it, I ended up with not only what I asked for but also something even better: one of the most significant mentors of my career.

The first of my two business careers was in marketing communications. In 1974 I was hired by the Mead Corporation in Dayton, Ohio, where I became director of Communications for the white paper group. I managed all advertising, public relations and internal and external communications for four divisions of this giant forest-products company. I had just gotten into the swing of things when Mead announced a corporate reorganization. Management decided that to better deal with a number of recent acquisitions, the company would transition to a decentralized business model. While my salary would stay the same, I viewed my shrinking responsibilities as something of a demotion. I pleaded my case that Communications should remain at its existing organizational level and lo and behold, the higher-ups agreed with me. One unanticipated result was that thanks to the reshuffling, I wound up reporting directly to the "top guy": the vice president of the Paper Group, Burnell Roberts. The day that decision was made turned out to be my lucky day.

Burnell had joined Mead in 1966 after earning a Harvard M.B.A. and gaining experience in public accounting and with some major corporations. By 1974, the year I joined the company, he had been named corporate group vice president. He ultimately went on to become chairman and CEO. As for me, I left Mead after a few years to begin my second career. But while I was privileged to work for Burnell for only a relatively brief period, our working relationship broadened me considerably. We never had a formal, stated mentor-mentee relationship but rather what was for me a very satisfactory boss-employee one. Burnell wasn't aware that I considered him a mentor until I approached him about writing this piece.

It was Burnell's highly effective management style that impressed me most deeply. I embraced it as we worked together and tried to emulate his technique after I moved on. To whatever extent I succeeded at that, I'm sure it contributed to my later business success.

The technique I refer to is sometimes called the Socratic method. It's based on the posing of thought-provoking questions. Because Burnell's scope of responsibility was so broad, he couldn't spend a great deal of time directly overseeing what I was doing. Instead of micromanaging me and my department, Burnell and I would meet monthly to discuss what I had accomplished in the past month and what I planned to accomplish in the month ahead. This afforded me a great deal of freedom to do my job and to grow in it.

He had learned the Socratic method in business school, then practiced and perfected it over the course of his career. As he told me recently, when he discovered how little he knew about certain subjects, he learned to rely on the skills of good people to drive the results required to achieve the company's goals in its highly competitive marketplace. While he experienced varying degrees of success using the Socratic method among different management disciplines, the process largely remained the same.

Typically, he would start off by asking about my plans, then question me as I described each step. As the questions and answers progressed, so would my thoughts about the wisdom of a particular course of action. But once we agreed on doing something there was no second-guessing. If I were to stray off an agreed-on path, he would let me know about it immediately. He recognized that mistakes were inevitable and taught me that it was vital to admit one's errors and correct things quickly. It was liberating to work in an environment where I had the freedom to make a mistake without the fear of being fired.

A typical review session with Burnell might have gone something like this: I say "might have gone" because, by necessity, I'm making this up. I can barely remember what I had for breakfast today, so recalling a conversation that took place 40 years ago is a stretch. But this is close enough to be an accurate rendition.

> BR: Tell me what you'll be working on for the coated printing paper division in the next few weeks.

> Me: I'm working with the ad agency to develop a new campaign to promote our products to annual report designers.

BR: What direction is the campaign taking?

Me: Well, it's still in the early stages but we're thinking about using a testimonial approach. We'll ask a few designers who specified our papers last year to say how happy they were with the finished product.

BR: That's interesting. Why do you think it would be successful?

Me: If we can show that some really high-end annual reports from big-name companies were printed on Mead stock, it will inspire other designers to specify our paper instead of our competition's.

BR: Has the testimonial approach been used before?

Me: I don't know. I'd have to research that.

BR: If it turns out that we've done it recently or that a competitor has done it, do you think that might dilute the effectiveness of the campaign?

Me: Possibly. But a good testimonial campaign is generally very powerful.

BR: Might some customers or designers who aren't asked to provide a testimonial feel slighted?

Me: That's a good point. I hadn't considered that. Maybe we should consider taking a different approach just to head off the downsides. I'll talk to the agency and we'll get to work on an alternate concept.

As you can see, it takes a great deal of discipline and patience on the part of an extremely busy manager to manage in this way. The temptation, when the boss has five more appointments lined up and the phone keeps ringing, would be to simply tell the employee what to do. This might—or might not—achieve the same result as the Socratic process, but it does nothing to develop the employee's critical thinking, much less to motivate them to innovate. Our conversations stretched my thinking, afforded me creative freedom, and pushed me to perform to a high standard. Sure, I made mistakes, but Burnell's searching management style helped ensure that I always learned from them.

Working under Burnell's leadership and among many bright and energetic people at Mead made my time there very satisfying. Then one day my father, who had acquired a small bakery machinery manufacturing business, asked me if I would consider coming to work with him. The incentive was that I would eventually take over and run that business. After a great deal of reflection, I decided to take that step, and my career with Mead Corporation ended after only three years. But I brought valuable lessons about management to this new stage of my business life, and many of the lessons came from my work with Burnell Roberts.

One day, a young engineer came to me and asked what he should do about a certain engineering problem. Not being an engineer, I had no idea. Instead of winging it and giving an answer, I started questioning him about alternatives. I ultimately asked him what he would recommend. He was visibly taken aback—clearly, he had never been asked that before. But after a bit of thought, he suggested the solution and I gave him the green light to try it out. That was the beginning of a true growth spurt for him professionally. Once he got used to the idea, he always offered a solution without being prompted. More often than not his suggestion was the right thing to do. The company progressed and grew and so did he.

Without knowing it, Burnell Roberts gave me a wonderful gift. As a manager I found pleasure in paying it forward when I could. In the process, with the help of an excellent staff, the business I had joined with my father grew significantly, and became a worldwide leader in the markets we served.

BOB ZIELSDORF graduated from the University of Notre Dame with a degree in communication arts and worked in marketing communications for over a decade. In 1977, he joined the Peerless Machinery Corporation, owned by his father Frank; in 2008, the much-expanded company was sold to Illinois Tool Works and Bob retired. Drawn from the 400-plus personal letters Bob and his wife Fran exchanged before their marriage, Bob's memoir, *Sealed with a Kiss: An American Love Story in Letters*, is a coming-of-age story, a romance, and a glimpse of an exceptional time in our nation's history. Bob and Fran live in Vero Beach, Florida; his favorite pastimes include golf, fly fishing, boating, and shooting (of the sport rather than the criminal variety). Find out more at www.bobzielsdorf.com.

Contributor Information

Boston-area resident **LEAH ABRAHAMS** is the creator and owner of Mixed Media Memoirs LLC, a publishing company. She is a personal historian, writing, editing and/or creating memoir books and oral history videos for her clients, some for private distribution and some for sale to the public. She also shows her fine art photography in Boston-area venues. Leah was born and raised in Chicago; she has a B.A. from Northwestern University and an M.A. from the University of Wisconsin at Madison. She worked in the public sector evaluating government-funded programs and then in market research in the financial services industry. Leah has been honored for leadership in voluntary organizations in her former community of Green Bay, Wisconsin and is a member of the Association of Personal Historians. Find Leah online at www.mixedmediamemoirs.com.

Originally from Raleigh, Reverend **J. DAVID BEAM** serves as the Senior Pastor at Pinehurst United Methodist Church in Pinehurst, North Carolina. David is a graduate of the Wesley Foundation at Wake Forest University and Emory University's Candler School of Theology. He has been married to Carolyn, a freelance medical and science writer, for over nine years and they have two young children, Adele and Joseph. In his free time, David enjoys Wake Forest sports, reading, riding his bike, traveling, watching movies, dining out, visiting with friends and family, and spending time with Carolyn, their children, and their high-maintenance dog, Sophie. Find many of David's sermons at www.pinehurstumc.org/sermons.

KIM BECKER is the founder of Hello Gorgeous! of HOPE, a nonprofit organization that restores in women the beauty that cancer steals. Kim has been in the beauty industry as a salon owner and national educator for more than 25 years. A fundraiser, educator, public speaker, consultant and the face of Hello Gorgeous!, Kim has received the Spirit of Women and Daily Points of Light Awards. Kim's books are *Hello Gorgeous!: A Journey of Faith, Love and Hope,* a Mom's Choice Award winner, and *I Promise to Put My Lipstick on When I Get There,* for women battling cancer. Kim and her husband Michael have been married for over 20 years and thrive in Indiana with their son, Seth, and a pug named Sam. Find out more at www.hellogorgeous.org.

KEN BENEDICT is Founder and Co-Director of the Center for Psychology & Education, PLLC. He is a Licensed Psychologist and Certified Health Care Provider in North Carolina. Ken's areas of specialization include psychological, psychoeducational, and developmental neuropsychological assessment of students from three years of age into adulthood; legal evaluations; parent and school consultation; adolescent development; and individual and family therapy. He has years of experience working with students with a variety of challenges and enjoys consulting with private schools and testing agencies. Ken's undergraduate training in psychology was completed at Dartmouth College; he received his master's and doctoral degrees from the University of North Carolina at Chapel Hill and completed clinical internships and postdoctoral training at Harvard Medical School/Massachusetts General Hospital in Boston. Ken and his family live in Chapel Hill, North Carolina. Find out more at www.cpsyched.com.

MARILYN BOUSQUIN is the founder of Writing Women's Lives™, where she teaches women who are done with silence how to free their voice, claim their truth, and write their memoir stories with confidence, craft, and consciousness. Her book reviews and memoir essays appear in *River Teeth, Literary Mama, Under the Gum Tree, Superstition Review,* and *Pithead Chapel,* and her essay "Against Memory" was a finalist for AROHO's Orlando Prize for Creative Nonfiction. Her memoir-in-progress explores the correlation between the female body, self, and voice. A broadside of Lucille Clifton's poem "won't you celebrate with me" hangs above her writing table, which is painted robin's-egg blue. Find out more at www.writingwomenslives.com.

HALE BRADT is a published author and retired physics professor who served on the faculty of The Massachusetts Institute of Technology from 1961 to 2001. During the Korean conflict, he served in the US Navy. He shares his parents' stories with insight, compassion, and a wealth of photos, documents, and records that bring their collective experience to life in *Wilber's War: An American Family's Journey Through World War II*, which is available in two editions: the trilogy, published as a boxed set, and the one-volume condensation, *Wilber's War (abridged)*. Find out more at www.wilberswar.com.

BARBARA ALANA BROOKS attended the University of Wisconsin and graduated from American University in Washington D.C. with a degree in elementary education. Barb's journey as a teacher, mom, wife, traveler and adventurer, along with her lifelong path of searching and exploration, have all enriched her life as an artist and writer. Her books include *Expressions of Spirit,* which depicts the richly soulful mandala art Barb has created over many years, and *The Coloring Journal: An Awakening Journey Through the Art of Barbara Alana Brooks,* which offers images of the mandalas to color coupled with additional tools for reflection and clarity. Barb lives in Florida with her husband Bud. Find out more at www.barbsartwork.com.

ROBIN LYNN BROOKS is a published poet and playwright whose art has traveled nationwide. She has an M.F.A. in Sculpture from the School of the Museum of Fine Arts in Boston. Her last body of work, *Earth Mothers,* is a series of life-size and larger women made of earth. She is also a book designer. The author of the poetic memoir *The Blooming of the Lotus: a spiritual journey from trauma into light,* Robin writes healing books, speaks, and leads workshops for women survivors. Robin lives in western Massachusetts on an old farm that borders the state forest. It was here that she found her first mothering—in the earth. The white pines behind her house shelter her. The lake in the woods is her temple. This was the place of nurturance that gave her the support to heal. Robin's website is www.bloomingofthelotus.com.

GRAYSON CHESSER is a waterfowling guide, conservationist, and decoy maker whose work, highly sought out by collectors, has been exhibited at the Smithsonian Institution and Cummer Museum among other venues. *Making Decoys: The Century-Old Way,* which Chesser co-authored with Curtis J. Badger, shares his decoy-making techniques as well as the carving traditions of

Virginia's Eastern Shore. He and his wife Dawn own and operate the Holden Creek Gun Club in Sanford, Virginia. Grayson Chesser has given back to the life of the Eastern Shore in a variety of ways: through his service as a game warden, his tenure on the Board of Supervisors of Accomack County, and his participation as a mentor/teacher in the Virginia Folklife Apprenticeship Program, which honored him as a Virginia Folk Master in 2004.

MARY EDWARDS is a composer, songwriter and sound designer whose projects range from recordings and performances "evocative of epic cinematic soundtracks combined with lyrical intimacy" (*Time Out* Magazine) to immersive environmental and architectural sound installations. Themes of temporality, impermanence, nostalgia, longing, childhood and the natural world are interspersed throughout her work. She has worked as performer or composer on a wide variety of film, theatre and television scores (BBC, PBS, The Learning Channel and ABC-TV); is a practitioner of the sound healing arts; and has lectured widely as a composer-in-residence on acoustic ecology, which studies music and the relationship between living beings and their environment, mediated through sound. Find out more about Mary's work at www.maryedwardsmusic.com.

Personal historian **KATHY EVANS** has been asking people to tell their stories to her since she was a child and writing since she learned how to make letters. Throughout her previous career in occupational therapy, she found herself drawn to learning the stories of her patients' lives. In 2001 she combined her interest in people's lives with her love of writing, and created Write For You LLC, which has produced more than 40 memoirs for clients since its founding. She has taught memoir writing as well as children's writing workshops. Kathy lives in St. Louis, Missouri; when not working, she likes to spend time with her family, garden, and watch the birds. Find out more at www.writeforyoustl.com.

A Phi Beta Kappa graduate of the University of North Carolina at Chapel Hill, **ANDY FOX** taught public secondary school special needs students and managed manufacturing and maintenance operations in two different industries before becoming a registered financial advisor. In that role, he served as senior vice-president for a top investment firm, specializing in retirement plans and financial planning. Helping one of his twins through a 13-month treatment program for life-threatening cancer at Duke Children's Hospital has given Andy a special interest in both the work of healing institutions and the importance of expressing and preserving personal legacy. Andy is a partner in Stories of You Books, which publishes stories that connect, in anthologies that endure, with impact that transforms. The father of three grown children, Andy lives in Pinehurst, NC with his wife Susan. Find out more about Andy and his work at www.storiesofyou.org.

―――――――――――――――――――――――――

RAYMOND HENGERER was born in Lackawanna, New York. Raised by Patricia and George Hengerer with an emphasis on a good work ethic and strong moral compass, he lived in the states of New York, California, and Georgia before finding his home in Vero Beach, Florida. Ray owns and operates Agua Vida Services, a full-service pool contracting company offering pool and spa services from building to cleaning pools. Agua Vida serves its community with the mission, "Give back to the community that gives to us," a motto that also reflects Ray's enduring personal commitment to supporting charitable and community causes in the Indian River County area and beyond. His pastimes include golfing, guitar playing, and enjoying sports and social life with his wife, the writer Linda Gordon Hengerer. Find out more about Ray and his work at www.aguavidafl.com.

―――――――――――――――――――――――――

Raised in Chatham, New Jersey, **JAMES R. HICKS, JR.** earned his B.S. in business from Bucknell University. He earned his M.B.A at the University of Maryland after being stationed as a U.S. Army officer at the Pentagon. Jim spent his career working at New York City financial services firms including Manufacturers Hanover Trust Company, E.F. Hutton and Dean Witter Reynolds, specializing in leveraged leasing and other tax-advantaged investments. The father of two grown children—who have 4 children of their own between them—Jim lives in North Carolina with his partner Carole and their two dogs.

SUE HOLBROOK is a wife, mother, grandmother, and lay speaker in the Florida Conference of the United Methodist Church. A native Floridian who describes her writing, speaking and teaching work as sharing "God's Glory...with a side of grits," Sue encourages women to find the inspiration and strength in their own God histories. Sue is the author of *Faith Breezes: Glimpsing God's Glory in Everyday Life*; she is currently working on a follow-up book, *Scattered Storms*, as well as a collection of stories drawn from Biblical figures. Find out more about Sue's book and speaking, and read her blog, at www.sueholbrook.net.

CYNTHIA HURST grew up in a large family in Detroit. She has worked as a bookstore manager, a lobbyist assistant for Lear-Siegler, and a procurement and contracts manager with the State of Michigan. After raising two sons in the East Lansing area, Cynthia married successful inventor Richard Hurst. They moved to Vero Beach, Florida, where they enjoyed a life dreams are made of and shared the adventures of writing and world travel prior to his death in 2015. Cynthia is the author of four books. The first two are travel memoirs. The second two, *The Diamond Project* and *The Platinum Project*, feature the sparkle and strength of women and men today. Next, she is contemplating an exploration of our search for spirituality called *The Star Project*.

DR. BILL KEETON received his M.D. degree from the University of Mississippi Medical School. He served in the US Air Force as Chief of Anesthesia and Chief of the pain clinic that he established at Westover AFB, Massachusetts. After serving as Chief of Anesthesia at DeKalb Medical Center in Atlanta for 15 years, Dr. Keeton became the founder and director of DeKalb Pain Center from 1984 until he joined Pain Consultants of Atlanta in August of 2007. A frequent lecturer on emerging and state-of-the-art pain management, Dr. Keeton is also the author of *A Boy Called Combustion: Growing Up in 1940s Mississippi,* which won an Independent Publisher (IPPY) award for best Southern-region nonfiction. Find out more at www.billkeeton.com.

FRANCES KING is a writer and editor with more than 30 years in journalism, publications planning and management, nonfiction writing, and editing. She fell into personal biography eight years ago, and began to help individuals and families preserve their memories in printed legacy books through her company, HistoryKeep. Building on a love of biography and story, and with many years as an interviewer, she has written or edited more than two dozen books and often teams with other personal historians as a developmental and copy editor. Francie has a B.A. in English literature from Denison University and an M.A. in social anthropology from Boston University. Find out more about Francie and her work at www.historykeep.com.

LINDA LEARY is a mother, grandmother, self-acclaimed "Boomer Babe" (that is, a female Baby Boomer with pizzazz), trained practitioner in restorative justice for youth and adults, and moonlight writer. For more information on Paula Underwood, visit www.learningpeople.org.

Born and raised in Florida, **GENE LEE** currently lives in Indian River County. His plans to become a lawyer were derailed when at the age of 13, inspired by Ernest Hemingway and James Joyce, he began writing stories. After many years of writing and publishing his poetry in literary journals, Gene returned to his first love, fiction. His novel *Men Without Hate* follows two men from the Raines family through two very different wars and home again. When not writing he enjoys fly fishing in the Indian River for the snook, redfish, and tarpon roaming those waters and maintains a voracious and longstanding reading habit. Find out more about Gene and *Men Without Hate* at www.geneleeauthor.com.

KEN LEVINE is an Emmy-winning writer, director, producer and Major League Baseball announcer. He is the author of plays including 2016's *Going, Going, Gone!* and books including the satirical novel *Must Kill TV; The Me Generation...By Me: Growing Up in the '60s; It's Gone...No, Wait a Minute!; and Where The Hell Am I?: Trips I Have Survived.* Ken has worked on *MASH, Cheers, Frasier, The Simpsons, Wings, Everybody Loves Raymond, Becker,* and *Dharma & Greg,* and has co-created his own series including *Almost Perfect.* He and his partner David Isaacs wrote the feature *Volunteers,* starring Tom Hanks. Ken has also been the radio/TV play-by-play voice of the Baltimore Orioles, Seattle Mariners, and San Diego Padres. The co-writer of the produced musical *The 60s Project,* Ken blogs at www.kenlevine.blogspot.com, which *TIME Magazine* named one of the Top 25 blogs of 2011.

DEBRA M. LEWIS graduated from West Point in its first class with women. She is a retired Army Colonel, a Harvard MBA, and a Combat Commander who led a $3 billion engineer construction program in Iraq. Chair of the Hawaii Island Veterans Day Parade, Deb is actively involved in the Hawaii Island Women's Leadership Forum and authored "Decisions Built to Last" in the book *Decisive Women.* Experts at addressing one of the greatest leadership problems in America—lack of employee engagement—Deb and her husband, Doug Adams, help others build stronger relationships and learn to achieve more. Find out more about Deb and her work at www.sunrisealoha.com.

BECKY LOAR is a Christian vocal artist who sings to bring the Lord's word to life. A native Floridian, Becky received her B.M. degree in Vocal Performance from Samford University in Alabama and her M.M. degree in Opera Performance from the Manhattan School of Music. Becky has performed with the Aspen Opera Theatre, Bronx Opera, New York Philharmonic and the American Symphony Orchestra, among many other ensembles. An active vocal adjudicator and clinician throughout Florida, Becky currently teaches on the voice faculty at both Jacksonville University and University of North Florida in Jacksonville. Her first CD is *Rise*. Becky resides in Jacksonville, Florida with her husband Victor and their children, Charlotte and Nathaniel. Find out more at www.rebeccaloar.com.

California transplant **PAT MURPHY MCCLELLAND** loves the art of autobiography, memoirs, and personal narrative poetry, which she herself writes. A member of the National Association of Memoir Writers and She Writes, Pat has published several children's books. She has taught creative writing in Los Angeles and also taught "Writing for Healing" at the University of California at San Francisco Comprehensive Cancer Center. Her poetry has appeared in journals including *blynkt, Caravel Literary Arts Journal* (where the poem referenced above appears), *Snapdragon Literary Journal, ARAS Connections: Image and Archetype, Altadena Poetry Review, Feile-Festa Literary Journal,* and *Atlas Poetica;* she is also the author of a chapbook, *Turnings,* and a piece in the anthology *Chronicles of Eve* (Paper Swans Press, 2016). She is currently revising a book-length prose memoir, *The Masks of Grief.* Find out more at www.linkedin.com/in/ patricia-mcclelland-53722336.

LYDIA MCGRANAHAN lives in Oregon with her family. She's a fitness instructor at a Salvation Army Kroc Community Center and a Level Ten gymnastics judge for the USA Junior Olympic program. She is currently working on a memoir about love, freedom, and bald eagles. Her writing reflects the determination and perseverance of an individual who refused to give up, even against all odds. This essay is her first publication. When she's not writing, she's backpacking in the wilderness with her chocolate Labradoodle.

Born and raised in Brooklyn, **JOHN MACKIE** grew up imagining himself wearing a Dodger uniform and playing third base. When the fantasy of youth faded into reality, he became a New York City policeman, discovering that he would rather be a New York City cop than a third baseman for any ball club….well, almost. During his 17 years with the NYPD, he was decorated over 30 times and awarded the prestigious Medal of Valor. Since work-related injuries forced him into early retirement, he has published five Thorn Savage novels. John's essay on the inspiration for the series appears in Stories of You Books' *Stories of Inspiration: Mystery Fiction Edition.* John now makes his home in Florida. Find out more at www.mackiej.com.

***

GLENN MARSCH has been a Professor of Physics at Grove City College since 2004, collaborating with F.P. Guengerich as a "hidden physicist" in the Department of Biochemistry at Vanderbilt University since 1999. He has a B.S. in Physics from Clemson University and a Ph.D. in Molecular Biophysics from Florida State University. He completed postdoctoral research in Iowa and California and served as Professor of Physics at Union University in Tennessee from 1996 to 2004. Since then he has lived in rural Western Pennsylvania with his wife of 30 years, author Cindy Rinaman Marsch, and they have four grown children. Glenn Marsch enjoys gardening, making wine with the fruit he grows, and photographing the beauties of creation. His work is displayed at www.flickr.com/photos/sphericalbull.

In her roles as motivational speaker, leadership coach, master facilitator and business consultant, **SUSAN MAZZA** works with leaders and their organizations to transform their performance from solid to exceptional. CEO of Clarus Works, Founder/Author of Random Acts of Leadership™ and co-author of *The Character-Based Leader* and *Energize Your Leadership,* Susan was named a Top 100 Thought Leader by Trust Across America in 2013 and 2015 and a Top 50 Innovator in Leadership in *Inc.* in 2016. Susan and her family live in Vero Beach, Florida. To learn more about Susan and her work, visit www.randomactsofleadership.com, which has been named among the Top 100 Leadership Blogs since 2011.

LISA NIRELL helps CEOs and CMOs accelerate growth and innovation. She's the Chief Energy Officer of *Energize*Growth® and the founder of Marketing Leaders of DC™ and Atlanta. Innovative companies such as Adobe, Gannett, and Hilton hire Lisa to gain fresh insights and launch breakthrough marketing ideas. She is an award-winning *Fast Company, Forbes CMO,* and *Huffington Post* expert blogger. She also authored *EnergizeGrowth NOW: The Marketing Guide to a Wealthy Company and the recently released The Mindful Marketer: How to Stay Present and Profitable in a Data-Driven World.* Download a free chapter and video bonuses at www.themindfulmarketer.com and find out more about Lisa and her work at www.energizegrowth.com.

JAY PARINI is a poet, novelist, biographer, and critic. His five books of poetry include *Anthracite Country* and *House of Days;* his *New and Collected Poems: 1975-2015* appeared in March 2016 from the Beacon Press. He has written eight novels, including *Benjamin's Crossing, The Apprentice Lover, The Passages of H.M.,* and *The Last Station*—the last made into an Academy Award-nominated film starring Helen Mirren and Christopher Plummer. Parini has written biographies of John Steinbeck, Robert Frost, William Faulkner, and, most recently, Gore Vidal. His nonfiction works include *Jesus: The Human Face of God, Why Poetry Matters,* and *Promised Land: Thirteen Books That Changed America.* Find out more at www.jayparini.com.

ANN PARKER earned degrees in physics and English literature before falling into a career as a science writer. The only thing more fun for her than slipping oblique Yeats references into a fluid dynamics article is delving into the past. Her Silver Rush historical mystery series is set in the silver boomtown of Leadville, Colorado in the early 1880s and has been picked as a "Booksellers Favorite" by the Mountains and Plains Independent Booksellers Association. A member of Mystery Writers of America and Women Writing the West, Ann lives with her husband and an uppity cat near Silicon Valley, whence they have weathered numerous high-tech boom-and-bust cycles. Find Ann online at www.annparker.net.

DR. PETER HAMILTON RAVEN is a leading botanist and
environmentalist and the President Emeritus of the Missouri
Botanical Garden in St. Louis. A frequent speaker on the need for
biodiversity and species conservation and one of the individuals
named as *TIME Magazine's* Heroes for the Planet in 1999, he is
the recipient of the US National Medal of Science, the
International Prize for Biology, the Tyler Prize for Environmental
Achievement, and a MacArthur Fellowship among many other
honors. Born in Shanghai before growing up in California, Dr.
Raven has been instrumental in the international project to
publish the English-language *Flora of China,* a comprehensive
catalogue of China's more than 31,000 species of wild vascular
plants that encompasses 22 volumes of text and illustrations.

CHRIS RINAMAN is a freelance trombonist in the New York City
area whose performance and recording work encompass jazz,
rock, Broadway and classical ensembles. He attended the
University of North Florida and the Manhattan School of Music
and has toured as lead trombonist and soloist with the Artie Shaw
Orchestra and the First National Tours of *In The Heights* and
Memphis in performances throughout US, Canada and Japan. He
also composes, arranges, and orchestrates for vocalists including
Deana Martin, Michéal Castaldo, Steven Maglio, and Giada Valenti
(in the PBS special *From Venice With Love*). As a former assistant to

Academy-Award-winning film composer Howard Shore, Chris was head score consultant for the world premiere of *The Fellowship of the Ring for Symphony Orchestra and Chorus* at the Hollywood Bowl. He has also composed the scores to several independent films and to commercials for Western Union and Staybridge Suites. Learn more at www.chrisrinaman.com.

ZOYA SCHMUTER, M.D. graduated from medical school in Gorky, Russia. Emigrating from the Soviet Union over 40 years ago, her family went first to Israel, where Dr. Schmuter worked in the pathology department at Israel's Beilinson Hospital. After three and half years, the family settled in the US. As a foreign graduate, Dr. Schmuter again took exams, did a four-year residency and served a one-year fellowship in Michigan. Ultimately settling in New York, she began a career as a medical examiner in the New York City Office of the Chief Medical Examiner. Dr. Schmuter is currently retired and resides with her husband in New York and Florida. Her four books include *Tales of a Forensic Pathologist* and *From Russia with Luck*. Find out more at www.zoyaschmuterbooks.com.

DELIA SEBORA is a native New Yorker and globetrotter. She teaches comparative literature, oral historiography, and world cultures. Still a ferocious reader, she believes that national and international travel deepen our understanding of ourselves, of being human, and of any books that we may happen to read. Delia has worked as an editor for academic, print and multimedia organizations. She completed graduate studies in California and now lives on the East Coast. She is currently writing a memoir about her insatiable pursuit of understanding, lessons learned and battles fought along the way.

Born in 1906, **G. LEDYARD STEBBINS** is widely regarded as one of the most influential evolutionary biologists of the twentieth century. His opus, *Variation and Evolution in Plants* (1950), is perhaps the best known among his seven books and other major scientific contributions and provided the conceptual framework for the emerging field of plant evolutionary biology. Stebbins' influence extended beyond botany, and with many colleagues he would fundamentally shape modern genetics and Darwin's theory of natural selection toward what is now acknowledged as the modern evolutionary synthesis. The material above is excerpted from his autobiography *The Ladyslipper and I*, which was edited after his death in 2000 and published by the Missouri Botanical Press in 2007.

LAURA STEWARD is a sought-after speaker, business advisor, radio host and author. After building and selling her highly successful technology services company she started Wisdom Learned, LLC, a company dedicated to educating leaders based on experience and wisdom learned in the trenches. Steward is the author of the award-winning #1 international bestselling book *What Would a Wise Woman Do? Questions to Ask Along the Way,* which was on the Amazon Women & Business bestseller list for over 90 weeks and continues to hit bestseller lists around the world. Through her weekly broadcast Radio Show, *It's All About the Questions,* keynote speeches, books, seminars, training and one-one sessions, Laura's mission is clear: help people get off autopilot and create amazing, successful lives. Find Laura online at www.laurasteward.com.

CATHY TRUEHART earned her diploma in nursing from the Worcester City Hospital School of Nursing, her B.S.N. in Public Health Nursing from Sonoma State University and her M.A. in Counseling Psychology from Leslie College in Massachusetts. Cathy has also completed certification programs in holistic nursing, Neuro-Linguistic Programming, reflexology and Reiki. Her book, *The Miracle of Hospice,* shares the insights and memories she gathered over many years as a hospice nurse. Recently retired from hospice work to care for and spend time with her mother Olive, Cathy lives with her husband Richard and Olive in Southampton, Massachusetts.

REBECCA TYNDALL developed her love of reading over 21 wonderful, literature-filled years. At the age of 17, she decided to let her outspoken opinions of books be heard, and launched a blog called *The Literary Connoisseur*. There, she speaks freely about books she loves, books that she doesn't love, books that have impacted her life, and books that have changed her world. Follow her ramblings on www.theliteraryconnoisseur.com and at The Literary Connoisseur on Facebook.

Regarded as one of the world's preeminent biologists and naturalists, **EDWARD O. WILSON** grew up in south Alabama and the Florida Panhandle, where he spent his boyhood exploring the region's forests and swamps, collecting snakes, butterflies, and ants—the latter to become his lifelong specialty. The author of more than 20 books, including the Pulitzer Prize-winning *The Ants and The Naturalist* as well as his first novel, *Anthill*, Wilson is University Research Professor Emeritus at Harvard and makes his home in Lexington, Massachusetts. Find out more about Wilson and his work at www.eowilsonfoundation.org.

BOB ZIELSDORF graduated from the University of Notre Dame with a degree in communication arts and worked in marketing communications for over a decade. In 1977, he joined the Peerless Machinery Corporation, owned by his father Frank; in 2008, the much-expanded company was sold to Illinois Tool Works and Bob retired. Drawn from the 400-plus personal letters Bob and his wife Fran exchanged before their marriage, Bob's memoir, *Sealed with a Kiss: An American Love Story in Letters*, is a coming-of-age story, a romance, and a glimpse of an exceptional time in our nation's history. Bob and Fran live in Vero Beach, Florida; his favorite pastimes include golf, fly fishing, boating, and shooting (of the sport rather than the criminal variety). Find out more at www.bobzielsdorf.com.

Acknowledgments

First and foremost, our profound appreciation goes to the 41 contributors who shared their mentoring stories in this volume. It quite literally would not exist without them, and to each and every one we extend our deepest thanks.

It takes a (virtual) village to create a book, and the talented team that worked on the production side of this anthology did impeccable work transforming it from manuscript to final product.

CJ Madigan of Shoebox Stories continues to bring her unique gifts to the design and production of this book as well as to the visualization of everything else "SoYou." We are eternally grateful and forever in her debt.

Cindy Rinaman Marsch proofread this volume with patience, skill, and care. Mikki Lusquinos and Chris Stefanovich brought pizza, cheer and assistance at a crucial moment. The cover photograph by Csaba Peterdi via istockphoto.com provided inspiration for not just this volume but this series. As always, Tom Leonard, Chad Leonard,

Cynthia Callander, and the rest of the team at the Vero Beach Book Center offer the inspiration of great author and book events and a model of what independent bookstores can be.

Citations and Other Information

References to the great majority of persons in this book use the subject's true name. In a very few instances, a pseudonym is used at the contributor's request.

The information about the figure of Mentor in the Preface comes from "Homer's Mentor: Duties Fulfilled or Misconstrued?" by Andy Roberts, originally published in the *History of Education Journal* in November, 1999 and readable via the website of Fred Nickols at www.nickols.us/mentor.pdf.

The hymns quoted in J. David Beam's essay are from the United Methodist Church Hymnal: #382, "Have Thy Own Way, Lord" and #515, "Hymn of Promise." Quotations from Scripture are from the New International Version.

The obituary of Dr. Steven R. Covey quoted in Andy Fox's essay was written by Douglas Martin and appeared in the *New York Times* on July 16, 2012.

The quotation near the end of Pat Murphy McClelland's essay comes from "The Dry Salvages" in T.S. Eliot's *Four Quartets.*

The work cited in Delia Sebora's essay is *When in Doubt, Communicate* by Ruth Minshull and Edward Lefson, editors, Scientology Ann Arbor 1969:1.

Copyright and Prior Publication

Grateful acknowledgment is made to the publications and blogs in which the following first appeared, and to the authors and/or publishers for giving permission for these works to be adapted or reprinted here:

Ken Levine's essay on Bruce Anson first appeared on the author's blog, By Ken Levine: The World as Seen by a TV Comedy Writer on April 3, 2016 under the title "My Mentors" (www.kenlevine. blogspot.com).

Lisa Nirell's essay on Diana Nyad originally appeared on the author's blog, Marketing Waves, under the title "Water Works: Leadership Lessons from Diana" on September 2, 2013.

G. Ledyard Stebbins' essay on Theodosius Dobzhansky is adapted from Stebbins' autobiography, *The Ladyslipper and I*, published by the Missouri Botanical Garden Press in 2007.

Edward O. Wilson's essay on William L. Brown was first read by the author on May 17, 1997. It appeared as "A Memorial Tribute to William L. Brown (June 1, 1922 – March 30, 1997) in *Psyche: A Journal of Entomology*, Volume 103, pp. 49-53, 2000.

About Stories of You Books

As "the anthology people," we at Stories of You Books capture, share and celebrate the truths that can be found at the intersection of many compelling stories.

As custom anthology creators, we help each client identify and use their own organization's many powerful stories to engage members and markets, honor contribution, inspire action, and build and preserve priceless legacy.

As anthology publishers for the retail market, we conceive, curate, and publish impeccable, enduring anthologies characterized by intriguing topics, accomplished voices, and broad readership.

In all of our work, we try to balance innovative big-picture vision with impeccable attention to detail, and connect diverse individual perspectives not just to each other but also to shared human needs, values, experiences and dreams.

Are you an individual with insight or expertise to share? An organization seeking to deepen your impact, now and forever? A reader ready for fresh perspectives? If so, we hope you'll make us part of your journey.

For more information, including upcoming publications and calls for submissions, please visit us at www.storiesofyou.org.

Opportunities for Editors and Contributors

Beginning in 2017, Stories of You Books will open some of its series to editorial proposals and some of its anthologies to contributor submissions. For information on upcoming editorial and contribution opportunities, please visit www.storiesofyou.org.

STORIES OF YOU BOOKS